WOOCOMMERCE
PLAYBOOK

THE UNDERGROUND PLAYBOOK FOR
CREATING AN ONLINE STORE

KIRAN R.K.G

Book Title: WOOCOMMERCE PLAYBOOK

Author: KIRANRAJ K.G

Published by KIRANRAJ K.G
Viraly kulathoor Uchakkada, Trivandrum, Kerala – 695506

This edition published in: 2019

ISBN 9781075508370

DEDICATION

To my dad, who helped me to become an entrepreneur.

To my mom, who supports and motivated me
through all of my crazy Ideas.

To the people all over the world who is hustling
to enter into eCommerce Industry.

CONTENTS

CHAPTER 1
SHOPPING CARTS

A shopping cart is a small piece of software that act as on-line store's catalog, and allows online shoppers to view, select or modify products, and purchase those products or services online.

Types of Shopping Carts

Hosted shopping carts are the eCommerce solutions which is hosted and maintained by the organizations who created them, If you like to host your online store on a hosted platform then all you need to do is to sign up to your chosen host and you're good to go, these hosted platforms give you free and premium themes (templates) to set up a completely new store without writing a piece of code. One of the widely used hosted shopping cart platform is Shopify but there are other options, too like Site123, BigCommerce, Volusion, Wix, 3dcart, BigCartel, and X-Cart Cloud.

Self-hosted shopping carts are 100% customizable shopping solutions that you host on your server and manage most of these solutions are open source and publicly available. This simply means that you download the software and run it your-self in your own server. Some popular self-hosted shopping carts are: WordPress with Woocommerce plugin, Magento and there are plenty of their options too.

CHAPTER 2
WORDPRESS

Wentence W ordPress is the popular open source platform to create your website. Total worldwide active websites are estimated at over 127 million and WordPress powers more than 75 million websites throughout the Internet, Yes - more than one in four websites that you visit are powered and managed by WordPress.

WordPress is a simplest open-source content management system [CMS] licensed under the General Public License [GPL]. Since WordPress comes under GPL anyone in the world can use and modify the WordPress core. A CMS is a tool which helps you to maintain and manage your website - like content without knowing how to coding.

Initially, WordPress was a tool which is used to create and manage blogs nowadays, with a large number of plugins and themes which are available you can create any type of websites out of it.

With WordPress, you can create eCommerce stores, Blogs, Business websites, Forums, Social Networks, Membership sites, Portfolios, resumes pretty much anything you can dream up.

Difference between WordPress.org and WordPress.com

WordPress.org is a self-hosted WordPress which is 100% customizable according to your needs you can download the open-source software from wordpress.org website and install it on your server to make your own custom website which is maintained and managed by yourself.

WordPress.com is a hosted platform which is paid service that is powered by the WordPress.org open-source software. It's simple to use. but you lose much of the flexibility of the self-hosted WordPress. There are lots of restrictions for plugins and themes in WorPress.com platform. Most of the time, when you hear "WordPress" that usually mean the self-hosted WordPress which is available at WordPress.org. If you want to own your website completely without any restrictions then WordPress.org will be the best option.

CHAPTER 3
WOOCOMMERCE

Woocommerce is a free WordPress plugin that adds eCommerce functionality to your WordPress website so you can have a fully functional online store up and running with just a few clicks.

Woocommerce powers more than 99% of WordPress eCommerce websites in the European countries. With over 27,000,000 downloads and millions of worldwide active installations, It's definitely the driving force behind numerous online stores.

WooCommerce provides basic store functionality right out of the box, it's a free plugin and it's available from the WordPress Plugin Repository or right from your WordPress dashboard.

CHAPTER 4
HOSTING REQUIREMENTS

Woocommerce can be hosted on any hosting platforms according to your wish. Hosting plays an important role in your online store's performance and speed. I had selected some of the best hosting service providers for woocommerce stores.

For new Stores hosting platforms like SiteGround and Bluehost will be best. Their basic plan starts from $3.95p/m.

For Growing Stores hosting platforms like Wordpress.com and LiquidWeb are the best fit. WordPress.com basic plan starts from $45p/m and basic plan of LiquidWeb starts from $69p/m. I personally recommend going for LiquidWeb for Growing stores.

For Enterprise/Large stores hosting platforms like AWS and GCP - Google Cloud will be the best fit.

CHAPTER 5
WORDPRESS HOSTING

I n this playbook, we will host our first online store in Google Cloud with the help of Cloudways. Cloudways offers a free trial for its services for a couple of days. In this chapter, we will cover how to host a WordPress website in Google cloud using cloudways.

Benefits of Hosting WordPress on Google Cloud

Google Cloud is one of the most sophisticated, reliable, and fastest cloud infrastructure. Just to give you an idea, big companies like PayPal, Twitter use Google Cloud for their hosing requirements.

Here are some of the reasons why you should host your WordPress website on Google Cloud.

Uptime According to a study on the performance of the cloud infrastructure providers, Google Cloud had a downtime of just 3.46 hours in 2014. This means Google Cloud Engine was available for more than 99.9% of the time.

Businesses such as big eCommerce stores, trading sites, and news sites rely heavily on optimal server uptimes and even the slight interruption in the service can cause serious monetary damage.

Speed We all know that Google runs the Internet, you have to be on top of your game if you want to rank at the top in Google SERPs and Speed is one of the most important ranking signals that Google uses for building and ranking website in the SERP.

Reliability Google Cloud uses the same infrastructure as Gmail and YouTube. When was the last time you experienced downtime watching videos on YouTube or sending emails in Gmail? Of course, you don't remember.

What this basically means is that by hosting your website on Google's cloud infrastructure, you are hosting on the most well-maintained hardware and data centers available.

The team behind Google Cloud works vigorously to improve its services automating configuration changes, use an extra layer of verification to discover any potential problems, and closely monitor the impact on the infrastructure due to modifications.

Scalability Google cloud servers are highly-scalable and can handle unexpected traffic spikes with ease. Using the scaling feature of the Google Cloud Engine, you can upgrade and downgrade the size of your server without changing the IP address.

Sign up for Cloudways

You can sign up for Cloudways and take your Google Cloud server for a 3-day test drive.

Now verify your email to complete the signup process. After you've successfully signed up, click the Launch button to initiate the server launch process.

Select your Application

Select WordPress choice from the drop-down menu and name your Application, Server, and Project.

Note: You have the choice of launching Cloudways Optimised WordPress, WordPress with WooCommerce, WordPress Multisite, or WordPress without any optimization.

Select your Hosting Server

Select Google Cloud Platform as your cloud server.

Select Server Size

Select the server size that best fits your requirements. Cloudways offers scalable WordPress hosting, which means you can always scale up/down your server from **Server Management** → **Vertical Scaling**.

Select Bandwidth and Storage

On Cloudways, you can select bandwidth based on your needs

to keep the costs to a minimum. You can also select separate storage sizes for database and application files.

Select Location

Choose the data center nearest to your target audience. Always make sure you're choosing the nearest data center, If the data center is near your audience your audience can browse your website more quickly and faster. For Google cloud, you have the option to host in 3 regions (USA, Europe, and Asia) and 11 different locations.

Launch the Server

If you're satisfied with the estimated cost of your selected Google Cloud server, just press the Launch Now button.

Now, wait for a few minutes while your Google Cloud server is getting ready. (normally it takes 7minutes)

Once the server is ready, go to Applications from the top menu bar.

Click My WordPress application.

To login to your WordPress website, go to **Application Management** → **Access Details** → **Admin Panel**. You will see the admin credentials (username and password) for your WordPress application. Click the URL, and then copy and paste the credentials to access the WordPress admin panel.

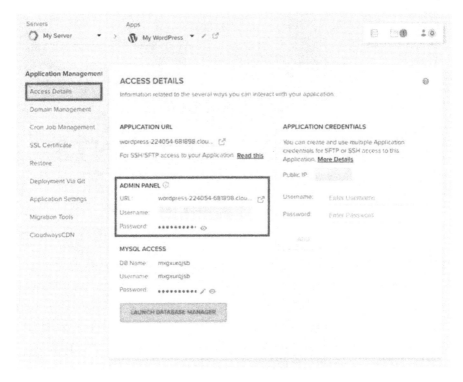

That's it! You have successfully launched WordPress on Google Cloud.

CHAPTER 6
SERVER REQUIREMENTS

T he first step to create an online store using woocommerce is installing WordPress, In the previous chapter we had discussed hosting and Installing WordPress in Google Cloud using cloudways now in this chapter we will discuss the Server requirements to install Woocommerce plugin.

Woocommerce Server Requirements:

1. PHP version 7.2 or greater.
2. MySQL version 5.6 or greater OR MariaDB version 10.0 or greater.
3. The WordPress memory limit of 128 MB or greater.
   4. HTTPS support.

CHAPTER 7
INSTALLING & UNINSTALLING WOOCOMMERCE

In the previous chapter, we had discussed the server requirements of the WooCommerce plugin. In this chapter, we will discuss Installing and Uninstalling Woocommerce, through the WordPress Admin Dashboard.

To install WooCommerce:

WooCommerce

WooCommerce is a powerful, extendable eCommerce plugin that helps you sell anything. Beautifully.

By Automattic

Install Now

More Details

⭐⭐⭐⭐½ (2,433)   **Last Updated:** 1 week ago

1+ Million Active Installs   ✓ **Compatible** with your version of WordPress

1. **Log into your WordPress site.**
2. Go to: **Plugins > Add New.**
3. Search for '**WooCommerce**'.
4. Select **Install Now** when you see it's by Automattic.
5. Select **Activate Now** and you're ready.

WooCommerce Setup Wizard

When WooCommerce plugin is successfully activated for the first time you will redirect to Woocommerce Setup Wizard.

Once you're redirected to the setup wizard, Select Let's go! to get started. Or select Not Right Now if you prefer to manually set up your WooCommerce shop manually.

The following wizard will help you configure your store and get you started quickly.

Where is your store based?

United States (US)

Address

Address line 2

City   State   Postcode / ZIP

Alabama

What currency do you accept payments in?

United States (US) dollar ($ / USD)

What type of products do you plan to sell?

I plan to sell both physical and digital products

☐ I will also be selling products or services in person.

Let's go!

There are two things to understand when uninstalling or removing WooCommerce from WordPress.

If you deactivate and delete the Woocommerce plugin from WordPress, you only remove the plugin and its files but all Your Woocommerce settings, orders, products, pages, etc... will exist in the database.

If you need to remove ALL WooCommerce data, including products, order data, etc., you need to be able to modify the site's wp-config.php file to set a constant as true.

```
define( 'WC_REMOVE_ALL_DATA', true);
```

Open your site's wp-config file (the main file of WordPress) and add the following line

define('WC_REMOVE_ALL_DATA', true);

above the

/* That's all, stop editing! Happy blogging. */ line.

Then you completely remove Woocommerce files and it's data's from your database.

CHAPTER 8
INSTALLING WORDPRESS THEME

We had installed Woocommerce successfully now it's time to Install a theme (template) on WordPress.

Uploading through the WordPress Dashboard

◆ Navigate to your **WordPress dashboard > Appearance > Themes and click the Add New button** from here you can search and select a theme for your shop If you like to purchase a premium theme you can purchase and upload it as .zip format through **Appearance > Themes and click the Add New button > upload**.

◆ Navigate to **Appearance > Themes** to Activate your theme.

Activate your theme key

If your theme was purchased from WooCommerce.com or from any other websites you need to activate the key.

After installing your theme, a notice will appear on your WordPress Dashboard to enter the key. please provide your key and activate it this will help you to receive automatic updates for your theme.

Troubleshooting

The package could not be installed. The theme is missing the style.css stylesheet.

If you're seeing this message, it's likely that you tried to upload a plugin or PSD file when trying to activate a theme.

The package could not be installed. PCLZIP_ERR_BAD_ FORMAT (-10): Unable to find End of Central Dir Record signature

This message normally means that you've uploaded a corrupt zip file. Download the theme again from WooCommerce.com and upload it to your website.

Can I switch from one theme to another without losing my data?

Customers commonly ask us if they will lose content when they switch from one theme to another. You will not lose content. Posts, pages, comments, users and settings are all saved into a database. If you are switching from one theme that has a custom post type built-in to a theme that does not have the same custom post type built-in, then this content will not display in your new theme. You will not 'lose' the content as this is still saved in the database.

For example, some of our themes have the 'Portfolio' custom post type built-in. If the new theme you are switching to does not have built-in support for the Portfolio custom post type it would not have the ability to display the content (that is saved in the database).

CHAPTER 9
WOOCOMMERCE PRODUCTS

W e had successfully installed Woocommerce and theme (template) for your store, now we have to add products for your store.

Adding a product

Before adding your first product, let's get familiar with how product categories, tags, and attributes work.

Product Categories

Product categories and tags work in much the same way as normal categories and tags you have when writing posts in WordPress. They can be created, edited, and selected at any time. This can be done when you first create a product or come back and edit it or the category tag specifically.

Attributes

Attributes can be added per product, or you can set up global attributes for the entire store to use (e.g., in layered navigation).

Attributes will help us to set up filters on your shop, filters help online customers to find products easily in your shop according to their needs.

Product Types

Before adding a product, the first thing to decide is what type of product you're adding to your online store.

Mainly we can add 6 types of products in Woocommerce.

Simple – covers the vast majority of any products you may sell. Simple products are shipped and have no options. For example, a book.

Grouped – a collection of related products that can be purchased individually and only consist of simple products. For example, a set of six drinking glasses.

Virtual – one that doesn't require shipping. For example, a service. Enabling this disables all shipping related fields such as shipping dimensions. A virtual product will also not trigger the shipping calculator in cart and checkout.

Downloadable – activates additional fields where you can provide a downloadable file. After a successful purchase, customers are given a downloadable file as a link in the order notification email. This is suitable, For example, for a digital album, PDF magazine, or photo. External or Affiliate – one that you list and describe on your website but is sold elsewhere.

Variable – a product with variations, each of which may have a different SKU, price, stock option, etc. For example, a t-shirt available in different colors or sizes.

Other types of products can be added by extensions (plugins). For example, WooCommerce Subscriptions adds new product types as does WooCommerce Bookings.

Adding a simple product

Adding a Simple product is almost similar to writing a post in WordPress.

◆ Go to **WooCommerce** > **Products** > **Add Product**. You then have a familiar interface and should immediately feel at home. 2. Enter a product Title and Description. 3. Go to the Product Data panel, and select downloadable (digital) or virtual (service) if applicable.

◆ Enter a product **Title** and **Description**.

◆ Go to the Product Data panel, and select downloadable (digital) or virtual (service) if applicable.

Note: Virtual products don't require shipping — an order with virtual products won't calculate shipping costs.

Product data

The Product Data meta box is where the majority of important data is added for your products.

General section

SKU – Stock keep unit (SKU) helps to keep products unique and formatted so it does not match any post IDs.

For example, post IDs are numbers so an SKU could be WS01. That could stand for WooShirt 01.

Price

◆ **Regular Price** – Item's normal/regular price.
◆ **Sale Price** – Item's discounted price that can then be scheduled for certain date ranges or a specific time period.

For example, The sale expires at 11:59 pm of the specified end date.

Inventory section

The inventory section allows you to manage stock for your product individually and define whether to allow back orders for your products. It enables you to sell products and allow customers to add them to the cart to buy.

Enable Stock Management must be selected in Products Inventory Settings; otherwise, only the '**Stock status**' option is visible in the Product Data Inventory box.

Options when stock management at the product level is disabled. You are responsible for updating the Stock Status.

Options when stock management at the product level is enabled.

1. Enter the Stock Quantity, and WooCommerce auto-manages inventory and auto-updates Stock Status as Stock, Out of Stock or On Backorder.
2. Select whether to Allow Backorders.
3. Low stock threshold – Enter a number upon which you are notified.
4. Tick the Sold Individually box to limit the product to one per order.

Shipping Section

1. Weight – Weight of your product.
2. Dimensions – Length, width and height of your product.
3. Shipping Class – Shipping classes are used by certain shipping methods to group similar products.

Linked Products section

Using up-sells and cross-sells, you can cross promote your products. They can be added by searching for a particular product and selecting the product from the dropdown list:

After adding, they are listed in the input field:

Up-sells are displayed on the product details page. These are products that you may wish to encourage users to upgrade, based on the product they are currently viewing.

For example, if the user is viewing the coffee product listing page, you may want to display tea kettles on that same page as an up-sell.

Cross-sells are products that are displayed with the cart and related to the user's cart contents. For example, if the user adds a Nintendo DS to their cart, you may want to suggest they purchase a spare stylus when they arrive at the cart page.

Attributes Section

On the Attributes tab, you can assign details to a product. You will see a select box containing global attribute sets you created (e.g., platform).

Once you have chosen an attribute from the select box, click add and apply the terms attached to that attribute (e.g., Nintendo DS) to the product. You can hide the attribute on the frontend by leaving the Visible checkbox unticked.

Custom attributes can also be applied by choosing Custom product attribute from the select box. These are added at the product level and won't be available in layered navigation or other products.

Advanced section

1. **Purchase note** – Enter an optional note to send the customer after they purchase the product.
2. **Menu order** – Custom ordering position for this item.
3. **Enable Reviews** – Enable/Disable customer reviews for this item.

Product Short Description

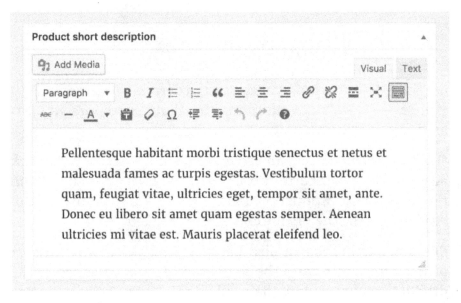

Add an excerpt. This typically appears next to the product image gallery on your product page, and the long description appears in the Product Description tab.

Taxonomies

On the right-hand side of the Add New Product panel, there are product categories in which you can place your product, similar to a standard WordPress post. You can also assign product tags in the same way.

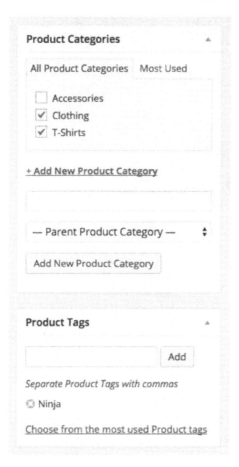

Setting catalog visibility options and feature

In the Publish panel, you can set Catalog Visibility for your product.

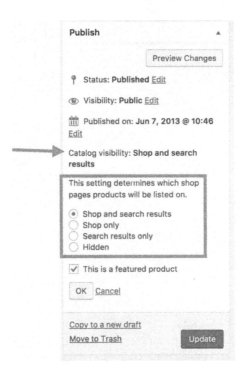

1. **Shop and search** – Visible everywhere, shop pages, category pages, and search results.
2. **Shop only** – Visible in shop pages and category pages, but not search results.
3. **Search only** – Visible in search results, but not in the shop page or category pages.
4. **Hidden** – Only visible on the single product page – not on any other pages.

You can also set whether the product is promoted in product categories, up-sells, related products as a Featured Product. For example, you could tick the Featured box on all the bundles you sell.

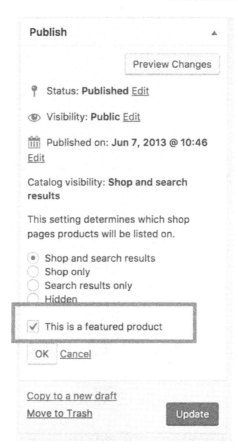

Other ways to set as Featured are described in the below section: Mark a product as Featured.

Adding a grouped product

A grouped product is created in much the same way as a Simple product. The only difference is you select Grouped from the Product Type dropdown

Create a Grouped product

1. Go to: **WooCommerce > Products > Add New**.
2. Enter a **Title** for the Grouped product, e.g., Back to School set
3. Scroll down to Product Data section and select **Grouped** from the dropdown menu. The price and several other fields will disappear. This is normal because a Grouped Product is a collection of 'child products', which is where you add this information.
4. **Publish.**

The Grouped product is still an empty group. To this Grouped product, you need to:

1. Create products and add them
2. Add existing child products Having the choice to first create Simple products and add them to a Grouped product later, or first create a Grouped product and add Simple products later gives you the flexibility to add Simple products to more than one Grouped product.

Add products to the Group

1. Navigate to: **WooCommerce** > **Products** > **Add New.**
2. Select the **Grouped** product you wish to add products to.
3. Scroll down to Product Data and go to **Linked Products.**
4. Select **Grouped Products**, and search for the product by typing
5. Click the products you wish to add.
6. **Update**
7. You can drag and drop to reorder the Grouped Products. Once you press Update, the new order will be shown on the product page.

Adding a Virtual Product

When adding a Simple product, you can tick the Virtual checkbox box in the product type panel.

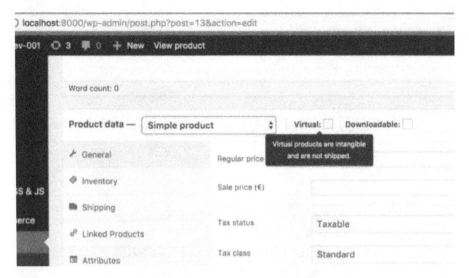

With Variable products, this checkbox is moved to each variation.

Enabling this disables all shipping related fields such as shipping dimensions. A virtual product will also not trigger the shipping calculator in cart and checkout.

Adding a downloadable product

When adding a simple product, you can tick the **Downloadable** checkbox box in the product type panel. This adds two new fields:

1. **File path** — Path or URL to your downloadable file.
2. **Download limit** – Limit on a number of times the customer can download the file. you can keep it blank for unlimited downloads.

For maximum flexibility, downloadable products also incur a shipping cost (if, for example, you were offering both a packaged and a downloadable version of a product, this would be ideal). You can also check the Virtual box if the downloadable product is not shippable.

Adding an external/affiliate product

Select '**External/Affiliate**' from the product type dropdown menu. This removes unnecessary tabs, such as tax and inventory, and inserts a new product URL field. This is the destination where users can purchase the product. Rather than Add to Cart buttons, they see a Read More button directing them to this URL.

Adding a variable product

Variable products are arguably the most complex of product types. They let you define variations of a single product where each variation may have a different SKU, price or stock level.

Example of a variable product is a T-Shirt which has different colors and sizes.

We will discuss more variable products in a separate chapter.

Duplicating a product

To save time, it's possible to use a product and duplicate it to create similar products with variations and other qualities.

Go to **WooCommerce > Products** and look through the list for a product you wish to replicate, then click Duplicate.

Deleting a product

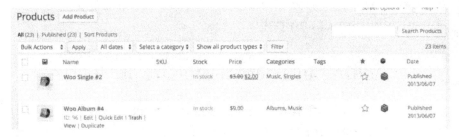

To delete a product:

1. Go to: **WooCommerce > Products**.
2. **Find** the product you wish to delete.
3. **Hover** in the area under the Product name and **click Trash**.

Mark a product as featured

To mark a product as featured, go to **Products > Products** and select the Star in the featured column. Alternatively, select Quick Edit and then the Featured option.

Filter or sort products

Filtering products

Use the Filter function to get a product count, view products by type, or see which products are On Backorder or Out of Stock.

1. Go to: **WooCommerce > Products**.
2. Select a **Category, Product Type** and **Stock Status**, or any combination of the three.
3. Click **Filter.**

Sorting Products

Sorting is different than Filtering, in that you can drag and drop products to re-order them.

37

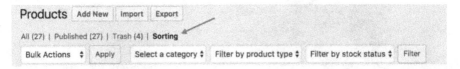

1. Go to: **WooCommerce > Products.**
   2. Select **Sorting.**
   3. Select a **Category, Product Type** and/or **Stock Status**, or any **combination** of the three.
   4. Click **Filter.**

You can now drag and drop products in an order to your liking.

Product ID

A WooCommerce Product ID is sometimes needed when using shortcodes, widgets, and links.

To find the ID, go to **Products** and hover over the product you need the ID for. The product ID number is displayed.

Allow backorders

Select whether to allow Backorders from the dropdown, if you are managing stock on a product. Use Advanced Notifications (separate premium plugin you need to purchase from woocommerce.com) to help notify someone other than the shop admin if backorders are placed.

To allow back orders, the Stock status must be set to In Stock even though the Stock Quantity is 0 or less.

CHAPTER 10
WOOCOMMERCE PRODUCT CATEGORIES

Product categories are the primary way to group products with similar features. You can also add subcategories if desired.

For example, if you sell clothing, you might have "t-shirts", "hoodies" and "pants" as categories.

How to add/edit product categories

Categories are managed from the **Products > Categories** screen.

Similar to categories on your posts in WordPress, you can **add, delete, and edit** product categories.

1. Add a Name.
2. Add a Slug (optional); this is the URL-friendly version of the name.
3. Choose a Parent if this is a subcategory.
4. Enter a Description (optional); some themes display this.
5. Choose Display type. Decide what is shown on the category's landing page. "Standard" uses your theme's default. "Subcategories" will display only

the subcategories. "Products" only displays products. "Both" will display subcategories and products below that.

6. Upload/Add Image (optional); Some themes have pages where product category images are displayed, so this is a good idea.

Storefront by default displays product category images on the homepage template.

Shop by Category

Clothing (13)   Music (6)   Posters (5)

Categories can also be **reordered** by dragging and dropping – this order is used by default on the front end whenever the categories are listed. This includes both widgets and the category/subcategory views on product pages.

The default category

Every product must be assigned to a specific category, so the products which are not assigned to a particular category will be automatically assigned to a default category and this default category is named as "Uncategorised" and this default category cannot be deleted.

However, you can rename the category. You can also switch the default category using the row actions underneath the category name, then the "Uncategorised" category can be deleted as it is no longer the default.

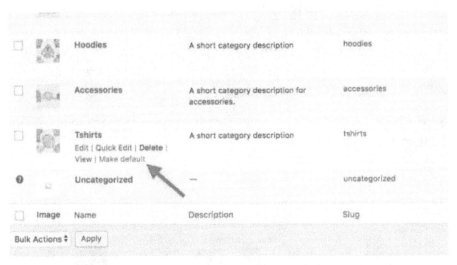

When you add a new product via **Products > Add Product**, you can select this new product category from the list.

Alternatively, you can navigate to **Products > Add Product** directly, and select **Add New Product Category.**

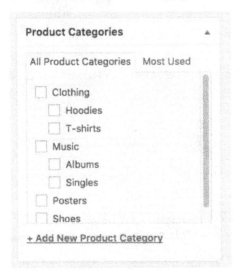

Product tags

Product tags are another way to relate products to each other, next to product categories. Contrary to categories, there is no hierarchy in tags; so there are no "subtags."

For example, if you sell clothing, and you have a lot of bunny prints, you could make a tag for "bunny." Then add that tag to the menu or sidebar so bunny lovers can easily find all t-shirts, hoodies, and pants with bunny prints.

Product attributes

A third and important way to group products is to use attributes. There are two uses of this data type that are relevant for WooCommerce:

◆ First is via WooCommerce widgets. "WooCommerce Layered Nav" works based on attributes. If you add this widget to your sidebar, customers can filter products in your store based on the attribute.

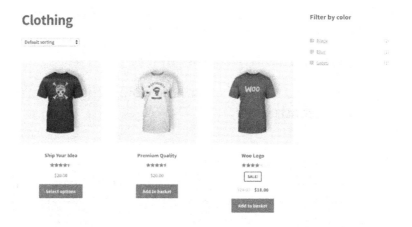

◆ Second is via variable products. To create a variable

product, an attribute must first be defined for the product. These attributes can then be used to make a distinction between different variations.

For example, if you're selling clothing, two logical attributes are "color" and "size", so people can search across categories for a color that fits their style and type and clothing available in their size.

Add/edit product attributes

Set Global Attributes

Navigate to: Products > Attributes to add, edit, and remove attributes.

Here you can quickly and easily add attributes and their terms.

◆ Add a Name.
◆ Add a Slug; (optional); this is the URL-friendly version of the name.
◆ Enable Archives if desired. If enabled, you can view a page with all products having this attribute. For example, if you have this enabled, and "black" is one of the options under "color", you can add

http://yourstore.com/pa_color/black/

to your menu to only display black clothing – pa stands for "product attribute."

◆ Select a Default sort order. Choose between "Name", "Name (numeric)", "Term ID" or "Custom ordering" where you decide by dragging and dropping the terms in the list when configuring the terms (see below). "Name (numeric)" is relevant if the values are numbers. If you select "Name", it sorts alphabetically with 1 and 10 preceding 2. If you select "Name (numeric)" it sorts based on a numerical value.

◆ Select **Add Attribute.**

The attribute is added in the table on the right but without values.

Select the "**Configure terms**" text to add attribute values.

Name	Slug	Order by	Terms
color	color	Custom ordering	Black, Blue, Green Configure terms
Numbers	numbers	Name (numeric)	– Configure terms

Next **Add New "Attribute name"**, where "Attribute name" automatically takes the name you gave the attribute in the previous step.

Add as many values as you wish. If you selected "Custom ordering" for the attribute, reordering your values can be done here.

Add global attributes to the product

Add the created attributes to your products.

Navigate to: **Products > Add** Product (or edit an existing one).

Select the **Attributes** tab in the Product Data. There you can choose any of the attributes that you've created in the drop-down menu.

Select **Add.**

If you selected a global attribute that you previously created, you can select terms that you added previously.

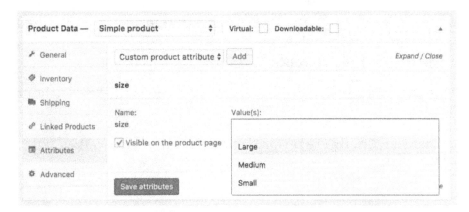

Add custom attributes

Alternatively, add an attribute you only want to use for one product. This would only be ideal if you have a product with unique variations.

Navigate to: **Product > Add Product.**

Select the **Attributes** tab.

Select **Custom product attribute** in the dropdown and follow the above steps.

CHAPTER 11
PRODUCT IMAGES

I mages are measured and set in pixels, for example, 800 x 800 pixels. Note that the first number is the width and the second is height.

Woocommerce recommends organizing your images in a folder offline and keeping a backup in case you need them in the future or mistakenly alter one and wish to revert to the original.

Types of Images

WooCommerce uses three types of Product Images for different locations and purposes:

1. **Single Product Image** is the largest image and refers to the main/featured image on your individual product details page.
2. **Catalog Images** are medium-sized images appearing in product loops, such as the Shop page, Product Category pages, Related Products, Up-sells, and Cross-sells.
3. **Product thumbnails** are the smallest images used in the Cart, Widgets, and (optional) Gallery thumbnails underneath the Single Product Image.

Adding Product Images and Galleries

Adding product images and galleries are options available on the right-hand side when adding or editing a product in your store from **WooCommerce > Products.**

Product Image

The **Product Image** is the main image for your product and is re-used in different sizes across your store.

Select **Set Product Image.**

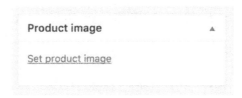

Select an existing image in your Media Library or Upload a new one.

Remove and Edit the product image if you'd like to change it, as needed.

Adding, removing and editing a product image is done in the same way as featured images for posts and pages.

Product Galleries

Product galleries display all images attached to a product through the Product Gallery meta box.

Create a **Product Gallery** using the same method as adding a

Product Image, but using the Product Gallery meta box.

Reorder Images in the product Gallery

Images in the product gallery can be re-ordered easily via drag and drop. Simply reorder your images by moving them around.

Remove Images from the gallery

To remove an image from the product gallery, hover over the image and click on the red "x."

Customer View

Once a product image and gallery have been added, customers can see them in your store.

CHAPTER 12
VARIABLE PRODUCTS

Variable products are a product type in WooCommerce that lets you offer a set of variations on a product, with control over prices, stock, image and more for each variation. They can be used for a product like a shirt, where you can offer a large, medium and small sizes in different colors.

Adding a variable product

Step 1. Set the product type

To add a variable product, create a new product or edit an existing one.

1. Navigate to: **WooCommerce > Products.**
2. Select the **Add Product** button or **Edit** an existing product. The Product Data displays.
3. **Select Variable product** from the **Product Data** dropdown

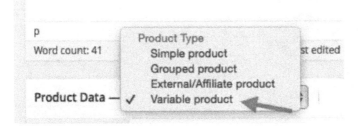

Step 2. Add attributes to use for variations

In the **Attributes** section, add attributes before creating variations — use **global attributes** that are site-wide or define custom ones specific to a product.

To use a global attribute:

1. **Select** one from the dropdown and **Add.**
2. **Choose Select all** to add all attributes to the variable product (if applicable).
3. **Tick** is **Used for variations** checkbox to tell WooCommerce it's for your variations.

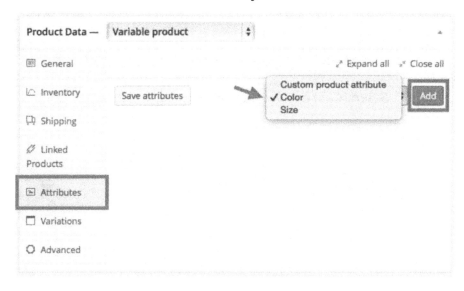

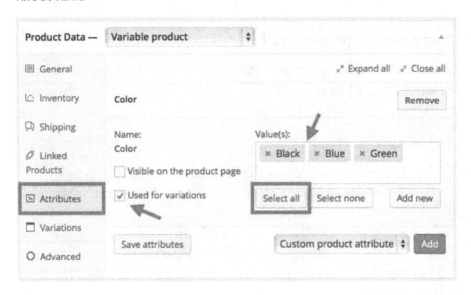

Custom attributes specific to the product

◆ **Select Custom product attribute**, and **Add**.

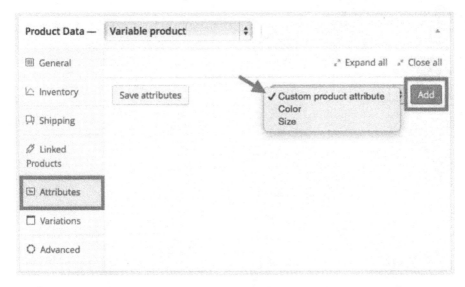

◆ Name the attribute (e.g. **Size**),
◆ **Set** values separated by a vertical pipe (e.g., **small | medium | large**)
◆ **Enable** the **Used for variations checkbox.**

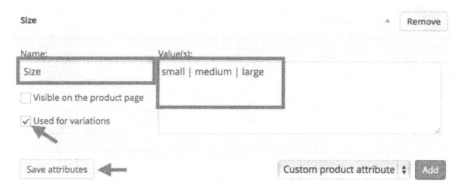

◆   **Save Attributes**

Adding Variations

Manually Adding a Variation

◆   **Select Add variation** from the dropdown menu, and click **Go**

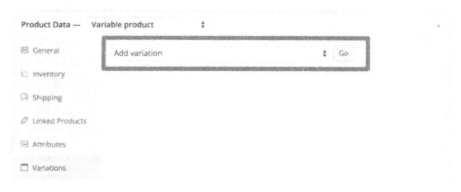

◆   Select attributes for your variation. To change additional data, click the triangle icon to expand the variation.

◆ **Edit** any available data. The only required field is **Regular Price.**

◆ **Save Changes.**

Editing Many Variations

If you have more than 10 variations, use the buttons to navigate forward and backward through the list. Each time you navigate to a new set of variations, the previous set are saved. This ensures that all data is saved.

Setting Defaults

Woocommerce recommends setting defaults you prefer on variations.

In the example, we have no defaults set, so users can pick any color and size right away from the product page.

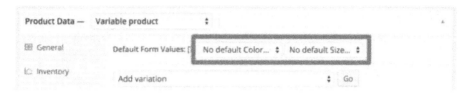

If you want a certain variation already selected when a user visits the product page, you can set those. This also enables the Add to Cart button to appear automatically on variable product pages.

You can only set defaults after at least one variation has been created.

Variation Data

Each variation may be assigned.

General:

◆ **Enabled** – Enable or disable the variation.

◆ **Downloadable** – If this a downloadable variation.

◆ **Virtual** – If this product isn't physical or shipped, shipping settings are removed.

◆ **Regular Price** (required) – Set the price for this variation.

◆ **Sale Price** (optional) – Set a price for this variation when on sale.

◆ **Tax status** — Taxable, shipping only, none.

◆ **Tax class** – Tax class for this variation. Useful if you are offering variations spanning different tax bands.

◆ **Downloadable Files** – Shows if Downloadable is selected. Add a file(s) for customers to download.

◆ **Download Limit** – Shows if Downloadable is selected. Set how many times a customer can download the file(s). Leave blank for unlimited.

◆ **Download Expiry** – Shows if Downloadable is selected. Set the number of days before a download expires after purchase.

Product data —	Variable product ⇕		▲
🔧 General	SKU		❷
◈ Inventory	Manage stock?	☑	
🚚 Shipping		*Enable stock management at product level*	
🔗 Linked Products	Stock quantity	5	❷
	Allow backorders?	Do not allow ⇕	❷
🎛 Attributes	Low stock threshold	0	❷
⊞ Variations			
⚙ Advanced	Sold individually	☐	
		Enable this to only allow one of this item to be bought in a single order	

Inventory:

◆ **SKU** – If you use SKUs, set the SKU or leave blank to use the product's SKU.

◆ **Manage Stock?** – Tick the box to manage stock at the variation level.

◆ **Stock Quantity** – Shows if Manage Stock is selected. Input the quantity. Stock for the specific variation, or left blank to use the product's stock settings.

◆ **Allow Backorders** – Choose how to handle back orders.

◆ **Low stock threshold** – Enter a number to be notified.

◆ **Sold Individually?** – Allow only one to be sold in order. (This is setting is used for the product itself. You cannot set a specific variation to only be sold once per order.)

Set Stock Status can be applied to all variations at once to In stock or Out of stock. Bulk-update under Variations.

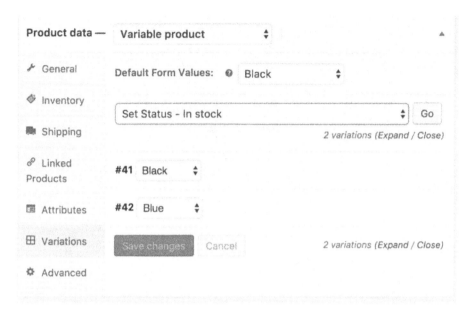

Shipping:

1. **Weight** – Weight for the variation, or left blank to use the product's weight.
2. **Dimensions** – Height, width and length for the variation, or left blank to use the product's dimensions.
3. **Shipping class** – Shipping class can affect shipping.

4.
5. Set this if it differs from the product.

Linked products:

1. Upsells
   2. Cross-sells
   3. Grouped

If the SKU, weight, dimensions, and stock fields are not set, then it inherits values assigned to the variable product. **Price fields must be set per variation.**

Adding an image for the variation

1. **Expand** the variation.
    2. **Click** the blue image placeholder (screenshot).
    3. **Select** the image you wish to use.
    4. **Save.**

#2488: Any color... ⬍   Any size... ⬍

SKU: [?]

☑ Enabled   ☐ Downloadable [?]   ☐ Virtual [?]   ☐ Manage stock? [?]

Regular Price: [$]   Sale Price: ($) Schedule
50

CHAPTER 13
WOOCOMMERCE PAGES

Upon installation, WooCommerce creates the following new pages via the Setup Wizard:

1. Shop– No content required.
2. Cart– Contains [woocommerce_cart] shortcode and shows the cart contents.
3. Checkout– Contain [woocommerce_checkout] shortcode and shows information such as shipping and payment options.
4. My Account– Contains [woocommerce_my_account] shortcode and shows each customer information related to their account, orders, log in details, etc.

Create default WooCommerce pages

Note: This tool will install all the missing WooCommerce pages. Pages already defined and set up will not be replaced.

Create pages

If you like to set up new pages yourself on your store or want to change the pages which are used for cart, checkout, My Account, etc. then you need to inform WooCommerce which pages to use.

To inform WooCommerce what pages to use for Cart, Checkout, My Account, and Terms and Conditions navigate to **WooCommerce > Settings > Advanced**.

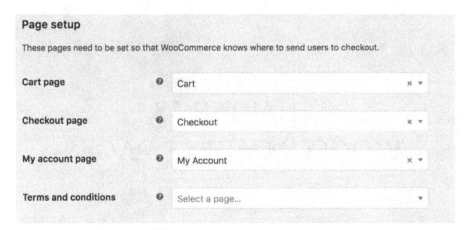

To inform WooCommerce what pages to use for the Shop page navigate to **WooCommerce > Settings > Products.**

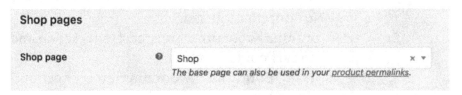

CHAPTER 14
WOOCOMMERCE ENDPOINTS

E ndpoints are essentially an extra part in the website URL that we detect and show different content when present without creating a separate page for that content.

For example, you have a **'my account'** page shown on the URL **yoursite.com/my-account.** When the endpoint **'edit-account'** is appended to the URL, making it **'yoursite.com/my-account/ edit-account'** woocommerce will show the Edit account page instead of the My account page.

This feature allows woocommerce to show different content without multiple pages and shortcodes, It also helps woocommerce to reduce the contents when it installs on your server.

By default the endpoints are already set up **WooCommerce > Settings > Advanced** in the Page Setup section.

Checkout endpoints

The following endpoints are used for checkout-related functionality and are appended to the URL of the /checkout page:

1. Pay page – **/order-pay/{ORDER_ID}**
2. Order received (thanks) – **/order-received/**
3. Add payment method – **/add-payment-method/**

4. Delete payment method – **/delete-payment-method/**

5. Set default payment method – **/set-default-payment-method/**

Account endpoints

The following endpoints are used for account-related functionality and are appended to the URL of the /my-account page:

1. Orders – **/orders/**
2. View order – **/view-order/{ORDER_ID}**
3. Downloads – **/downloads/**
4. Edit account (and change password) – **/edit-account/**
5. Addresses – **/addresses/**
6. Payment methods – **/payment-methods/**
7. Lost password – **/lost-password/**
8. Logout – **/customer-logout/**

Customizing endpoint URLs

The URL for each endpoint can be customized in **WooCommerce > Settings > Advanced** in the Page Setup section.

Ensure that they are unique to avoid conflicts. If you encounter issues with 404s, go to **Settings > Permalinks** and save to flush the rewrite rules.

Using endpoints in menu

If you want to include an endpoint in your menus, you need to use the Links section:

Enter the full URL of the endpoint and then insert that into your menu.

Remember that some endpoints, such as **view-order,** require an order ID to work. Woocommerce doesn't recommend adding these endpoints to your menus. These pages can instead be accessed via the **my-account** page.

CHAPTER 15
WOOCOMMERCE SETTINGS

I n this chapter, we will discuss more how to configure woocommerce general settings.

To get started to navigate to **Woocommerce > Settings**

General Settings

Store address

Store address will define your shop's address, country and state (i.e, Where you're shop is based as a seller) This information will help woocommerce to determine default tax rates and customer locations.

Selling Locations

Here you can Choose to **sell to all countries**. You can also select multiple specific countries or states according to your needs.

Shipping Locations

Here you can select shipping to those countries you sell your products. You can disable shipping & all shipping-related functionalities.

Default Customer Address

Choose the location we assume site visitors are in, before they enter it, to calculate tax and shipping.

1. Shop base address tells the system to assume they are in the same location as your shop.
2. No address gives them no location, so no taxes are calculated until they provide an address.
3. Geolocate address verifies where their current location and calculate taxes accordingly.
4. Geolocate with the page caching support is the same as above, but does the geolocation via Ajax. You may notice your website URLs have a ?v=xxxxx appended to them. This is normal to prevent static caching of prices.

Products Settings

In product settings, we can set how a product can be displayed, Image size, Inventory, and downloadable products settings.

In the **General** section, there are **Shop Pages, Measurements and Reviews**, this will help you to control checkout settings, select units of measurement, and enable/disable product reviews and ratings.

Navigate to: **WooCommerce > Settings > Products > General**

General | Inventory | Downloadable products

Shop pages

Shop page ❷ Shop   x ▾

The base page can also be used in your product permalinks.

Add to cart behaviour ☐ Redirect to the cart page after successful addition

☑ Enable AJAX add to cart buttons on archives

Placeholder image ❷ Enter attachment ID or URL to an image

Measurements

Weight unit ❷ oz ▾

Dimensions unit ❷ in ▾

Reviews

Enable reviews ☑ Enable product reviews

☑ Show "verified owner" label on customer reviews

☐ Reviews can only be left by "verified owners"

Product ratings ☑ Enable star rating on reviews

☑ Star ratings should be required, not optional

[Save changes]

Shop Page

Here you can select which page you need to use as the default shop page. Need not be the Shop page that WooCommerce installed you can create your own custom shop pages, or can be skipped if you use another method to display products.

Add to cart behavior

Here you select how your shop should behave when a customer

adds products to the cart. 1. Redirect to cart page after successful addition – Automatically takes the customer to the cart page upon adding a product. 2. Enable Ajax to add to cart buttons on archives – Adds the 'Add to Cart' option to shop archive pages.

Placeholder Image

Set a default 'placeholder' image to appear on the front end when no other image is available. This could be your brand logo or an image of a signature product or service.

Measurements

Select a unit of measurement for weight and dimension of products from the dropdown menu.

Reviews

Here you can Enable and control reviews which appear in products details page. Reviews are highly important in an online shop, it is social proof which helps you for more sales and conversions.

To Enable Reviews

1. Enable product reviews
2. you can select whether to display if reviewer bought the product or not.
3. Control if anyone can leave a review or only buyers

Product Ratings

1. Enable stars on reviews.
2. Select whether it's required or optional

Inventory Options

To edit your shop's inventory options, navigate to: **WooCommerce > Settings > Products > Inventory.**

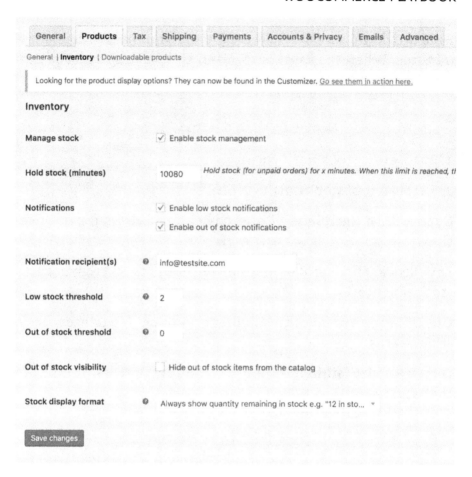

Select whether to enable stock management. If selected, you have these options:

Manage stock

1. **Enable** stock management – Inventory for physical products is auto-managed. You enter quantity, and WooCommerce subtracts items as sales are made, displaying: Stock, Out of Stock or On Backorder.

2. Disable (box left unticked) – Inventory and status for physical products must be entered manually. You can still Enable Stock Management on a per-product level if desired.

Hold Stock (minutes) – Hold products (for unpaid orders) for X minutes. When the limit is reached, the pending order is canceled. Leave blank to disable.

Notifications

1. Enable low stock notifications

2. Enable out of stock notifications

Notification Recipient – Enter the email address for notifications.

Low Stock Threshold – Number of products to trigger a low stock notification

Out Of Stock Threshold – Number of products to trigger out of stock status.

Out Of Stock Visibility – Choose to hide out of stock items from the catalog.

Stock Display Format

1. Always show stock – "12 in stock"

2. Only show stock when low – "Only 2 left in stock" vs. "In stock"

3. Never show amount

Downloadable Products

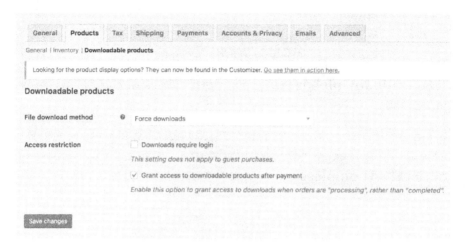

Navigate to: **WooCommerce > Settings > Products > Downloadable products**.

File Download Method

Controls how your store provides downloadable files to purchasers.

Force Downloads – Files are 'forced' to download via a PHP script. Files are not accessible to anyone but purchasers, and direct links are hidden.

X-Accel-Redirect/X-Sendfile – Similar to 'forced' above, but it has better performance and can support larger files. It requires that your hosting provider supports either X-Sendfile or X-Accel-Redirect, so you need to check with them first.

Redirect only – A download URL links the user to the file. Files are not protected from outside access.

Most stores should use one of the first two methods to keep files safe from outside access. The redirect should only be used if you encounter problems or don't mind downloads being non-secure.

Access Restriction

1. Select if downloads require a login – Does not apply to guest purchases.

2. Grant access to downloadable products after payment – Enable to grant access to downloads when orders are Processing, rather than Completed.

Shipping Settings

Navigate to: **WooCommerce > Settings > Shipping**.

The main shipping settings screen is for Shipping Zones. Think of a shipping zone as a geographic region where a certain set of shipping methods and their rates apply.

We will discuss more Shipping Zones in coming Chapters.

Shipping Options

| General | Products | Tax | **Shipping** | Payments | Accounts & Privacy | Emails | Advanced |

Shipping zones | **Shipping options** | Shipping classes | Free shipping (legacy)

Shipping options

Calculations — ✓ Enable the shipping calculator on the cart page

☐ Hide shipping costs until an address is entered

Shipping destination ❷ ○ Default to customer shipping address

◉ Default to customer billing address

○ Force shipping to the customer billing address

Debug mode — ☐ Enable debug mode

Enable shipping debug mode to show matching shipping zones and to bypass shipping rate cache.

Save changes

Shipping Calculations

1. Enable the shipping calculator on the cart page

2. Hide shipping costs until an address is entered

Shipping Destination

Ship to the billing address or customer shipping address by default or only ship to the user's billing address.

Debug Mode

Enable for troubleshooting purposes.

Accounts and Privacy Settings

Navigate to **WooCommerce > Settings > Accounts** and Privacy to control options relating to customer accounts and data retention.

1. 1. Allow customers to place orders without an account – Allows customers to check out without creating an account. Orders will not be tied to a user account in WordPress.
2. 2. Allow customers to log into an existing account during checkout – This displays a login form and prompts on the checkout page if the customer is not already logged in.

1. 1. Allow customers to place orders without an account – Allows customers to check out without creating an account. Orders will not be tied to a user account in WordPress.
2. 2. Allow customers to log into an existing account during checkout – This displays a login form and prompts on the checkout page if the customer is not already logged in.

Note: If you had not enabled the guest checkout on your shop, Google will not approve your Google Merchant Center account and Google Ads account. So, I recommend everyone to enable guest checkout on your online shop.

Account Creation

1. Allow customers to create an account during checkout
2. Allow customers to create an account on the My account page
3. Automatically generate username from customer email – If this is disabled, there will be an input box for the user to create their own username.
4. Automatically generate customer password – If this is disabled, there will be an input box for the user to create their own password. Note that while the password strength notification will be displayed, customers can choose any password so as to not limit conversions.

Account erasure requests

Remove personal data from orders – WordPress 4.9 allows you to remove personal data on request. When doing this, if you enable this option, user data will also be removed from your orders if they belong to the user being erased.

Remove access to downloads – WordPress 4.9 allows you to remove personal data on request. When doing this, if you enable this option, download data will also be removed if it belongs to the user being erased. The erased user will no longer have access to any purchased downloads if this happens.

Email Settings

Options available to edit email settings and templates.

Navigate to: **WooCommerce > Settings > Emails.**

Email Notifications

For each WooCommerce email listed, it's possible to configure your settings (optional).

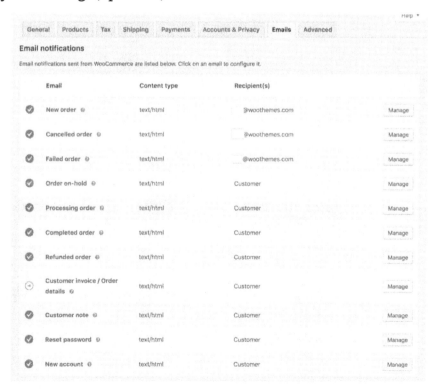

Email Sender Options

Set the 'From' name and email address for the sender.

Email Templates

This section lets you customize WooCommerce emails.

Email template

This section lets you customize the WooCommerce emails. Click here to preview your email template.

Header image	❷	N/A
Footer text	❷	https:// [____] mystagingwebsite.com
Base color	❷	▉ #557da1
Background color	❷	#f5f5f5
Body background color	❷	#fdfdfd
Body text color	❷	▉ #505050

Save changes

Header Image

Enter the URL of an image you want to show in the email header. You can upload an image via the Add

Email and Text

1. Base Color – Color for WooCommerce email templates.
2. Background Color – Background color for WooCommerce email templates.

3. Email Body Background Color – Main body background color.

4. Email Body Text Color – Main body text color.

For more advanced control, copy the **woocommerce/templates/emails/** folder to **yourchildtheme/woocommerce/emails/**.

Note: I personally recommend to keep all your changes on your child theme so that you will not lose any changes you made when you update your theme to the latest version.

CHAPTER 16
SHIPPING ZONES

T o set up shipping in WooCommerce, first we need to set up shipping zones, then add methods to those zones, and lastly, rates to your methods. You can create as many zones as you like, and add multiple methods and rates to each zone.

Shipping Zones

A **Shipping Zone** is a geographical area to which you ship items (physical products). You can get as specific as you need, right down to regions and zip codes, or you can leave it more general – whichever suits you best.

Customers only see the methods available for their address and corresponding zone. **Each customer matches only one zone.** Add as many zones as you need, with each zone containing multiple shipping methods.

Adding & Managing Zones

To set up shipping zones, go to **WooCommerce > Settings > Shipping**. If you don't see Shipping as an option, go back to **WooCommerce > General** and take a look at settings at Shipping

Locations – you may need to enable shipping settings there!

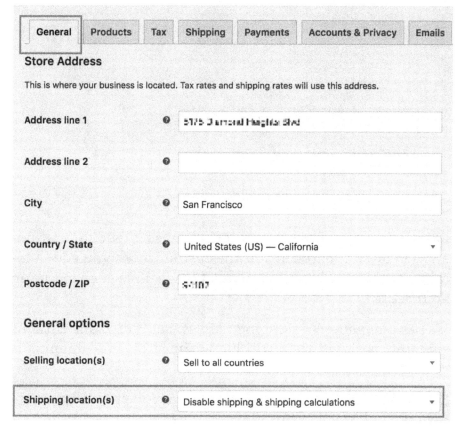

The first time you visit **WooCommerce > Settings > Shipping**, there is a prompt to add a new zone and a default zone.

A shipping zone is a geographic region where a certain set of shipping methods and rates apply.

For example:

- Local zone = California ZIP 90210 = Local pickup
- US domestic zone = All US states = Flat rate shipping
- Europe zone = Any country in Europe = Flat rate shipping

Add as many zones as you need – customers will only see the methods available for their address.

Add shipping zone

Locations not covered by your other zones is used for customers who do not match any of the custom zones you add. Adding methods to this zone is completely optional, depending on your needs. '

If a customer enters a shipping address that is in a zone without shipping methods, they will be informed that no shipping is available.

Since zones match from top to bottom, you can also exclude regions from shipping by adding a zone for that region and assigning no shipping methods to it.

Adding a new zone

◆ Navigate to: WooCommerce > Shipping > Shipping Zones.
◆ Click the Add shipping zone button at the top.

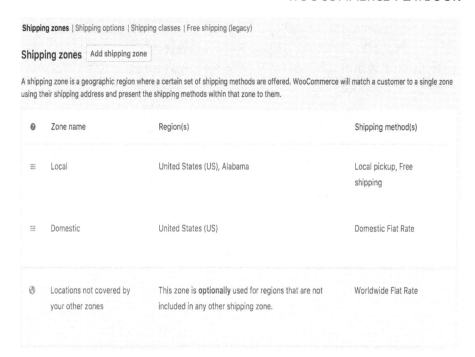

Shipping zones | Shipping options | Shipping classes | Free shipping (legacy)

Shipping zones   Add shipping zone

A shipping zone is a geographic region where a certain set of shipping methods are offered. WooCommerce will match a customer to a single zone using their shipping address and present the shipping methods within that zone to them.

	Zone name	Region(s)	Shipping method(s)
☰	Local	United States (US), Alabama	Local pickup, Free shipping
☰	Domestic	United States (US)	Domestic Flat Rate
⊕	Locations not covered by your other zones	This zone is **optionally** used for regions that are not included in any other shipping zone.	Worldwide Flat Rate

◆ Enter a descriptive Zone Name, and select Zone Regions that apply. Regions can consist of: a) Countries, b) States, c) Continents.

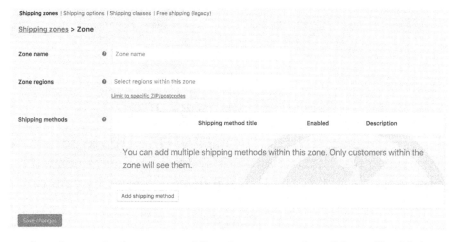

Shipping zones | Shipping options | Shipping classes | Free shipping (legacy)

Shipping zones > Zone

Zone name	❷	Zone name

| Zone regions | ❷ | Select regions within this zone |
| | | Limit to specific ZIP/postcodes |

Shipping methods ❷

	Shipping method title	Enabled	Description

You can add multiple shipping methods within this zone. Only customers within the zone will see them.

Add shipping method

Save changes

◆ Select **Limit to specific zip/postcodes** (if applicable) to further narrow which customers match this zone. For example, you can set a local zone with a specific set of postcodes (one per line); a range of postcodes (e.g. 90210...99000), or use wildcards (e.g. CB23*).

◆ **Select** which **Shipping Methods** are available to this zone.

◆ **Save changes.**

In the below example we created three zones – Local, Domestic, and North America to demonstrate how zones can be set up.

Shipping zones | Shipping options | Shipping classes | Free shipping (legacy)

Shipping zones Add shipping zone

A shipping zone is a geographic region where a certain set of shipping methods are offered. WooCommerce will match a customer to a single zone using their shipping address and present the shipping methods within that zone to them.

❼	Zone name	Region(s)	Shipping method(s)
≡	Local	United States (US), Alabama	Local pickup, Free shipping
≡	Domestic	United States (US)	Domestic Flat Rate
≡	North America	Canada, United States (US), United States (US) Virgin Islands, United States (US) Minor Outlying Islands	Flat rate
⊗	Locations not covered by your other zones	This zone is **optionally** used for regions that are not included in any other shipping zone.	Worldwide Flat Rate

Sorting Shipping Zones

Shipping zones match customer address from top to bottom — **the first to match the customer address is always used**. If no custom zones match, then **Locations not covered by your other zones** is used.

To sort and reorder zones:

1. Navigate to: **WooCommerce > Shipping > Shipping Zones.**
2. **Hover and click** on the far left handles. A four-point

icon appears on the screen.

3. **Drag and drop.**
4. **Save changes.**

Editing shipping zones

Shipping zones Add shipping zone

A shipping zone is a geographic region where a certain set of shipping methods are offered. WooCommerce will match a customer to a single zone using their shipping address and present the shipping methods within that zone to them.

	Zone name	Region(s)	Shipping method(s)
☰	Local	California, 90210	Local pickup, Free shipping
	Edit Delete		

To edit a shipping zone:

1. Go to: **WooCommerce > Shipping > Shipping Zones.**
2. **Hover** over **Zone Name**, and the option to **Edit** and **Delete** appear.
3. Select **Edit**, and a screen appears so you can change the name, regions or shipping methods.
4. **Save changes.**

The Locations not covered by your other zones section cannot be moved, renamed or deleted because it acts as a default when no other zones apply.

To delete a shipping zone:

1. Navigate to: **WooCommerce > Shipping > Shipping Zones.**
2. **Hover** over **Zone Name**, and the option to **Edit** and **Delete** appear.
3. Select **Delete**, and the Shipping Zone is deleted.

Adding Shipping Methods to Zones

To add a shipping method to an existing Shipping Zone:

◆ Navigate to: **WooCommerce > Shipping > Shipping Zones.**

◆ **Hover** over the **Shipping Zone** you wish to change, and select **Edit.**

◆ Scroll down to Shipping Methods on the screen that appears.

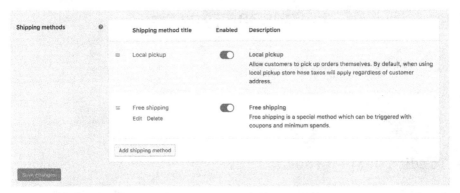

◆ **Disable** an existing **Shipping Method** by using the button. Or select the **Add Shipping method** to use a different one.

◆ **Save changes.**

Removing Shipping Methods from Zones

To remove a shipping method from a Shipping Zone:

◆ Navigate to: **WooCommerce > Shipping > Shipping Zones**.

◆ **Hover** over the **Shipping Zone** you wish to change, and select **Edit.**

◆ Scroll down to **Shipping Methods** on the screen that appears.

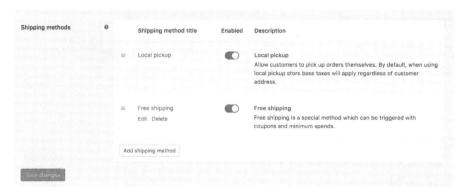

◆ Hover over the Shipping Method you wish to remove, and select Delete.

◆ **Save changes.**

Control the Shipping Method Selected by Default

The default Shipping Method for customers is the top listed, enabled shipping method in the zone that they match.

In this screenshot example, Local Pickup is chosen for a customer that matched the Local Shipping Zone.

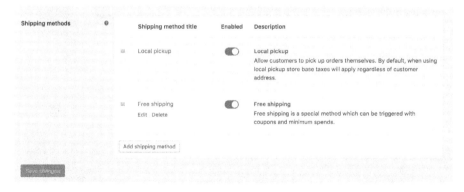

Drag and drop to reorder shipping methods using the handles on the left, then **Save Changes.**

You can also control how shipping methods are ordered in the cart page, on the same screen. All the selected shipping methods will be sorted in the cart page, in the same order you followed, to arrange them in this screen.

For customers matching the Local shipping zone parameters, shipping methods appear in the cart in the same.

Your order

PRODUCT	TOTAL
Premium Quality × **1**	$20.00
Ship Your Idea – Green × **1**	$20.00
Subtotal	$40.00
Shipping	• ◉ Local pickup • ○ Free shipping
Total	**$40.00** (includes $2.62 Tax)

How Zones Work for Customers

Using these shipping zones and methods:

Shipping zones | Shipping options | Shipping classes | Free shipping (legacy)

Shipping zones [Add shipping zone]

A shipping zone is a geographic region where a certain set of shipping methods are offered. WooCommerce will match a customer to a single zone using their shipping address and present the shipping methods within that zone to them.

	Zone name	Region(s)	Shipping method(s)
≡	Local	United States (US), Alabama	Local pickup, Free shipping
≡	Domestic	United States (US)	Domestic Flat Rate
≡	North America	Canada, United States (US), United States (US) Virgin Islands, United States (US) Minor Outlying Islands	Flat rate
⊛	Locations not covered by your other zones	This zone is **optionally** used for regions that are not included in any other shipping zone.	Worldwide Flat Rate

1. In the 90210 zip code in California, I offer Local Pickup and Free Shipping.

2. In the United States, I offer a Domestic Flat Rate.

3. In Canada and U.S. regions, I offer a different Flat Rate.

This is what your customers would see if they use the Calculate Shipping option:

CALIFORNIAN CUSTOMER

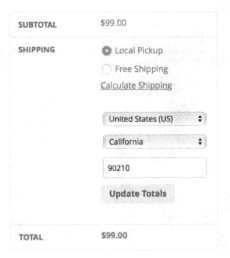

NON-CALIFORNIAN, U.S. CUSTOMER

INTERNATIONAL CUSTOMER

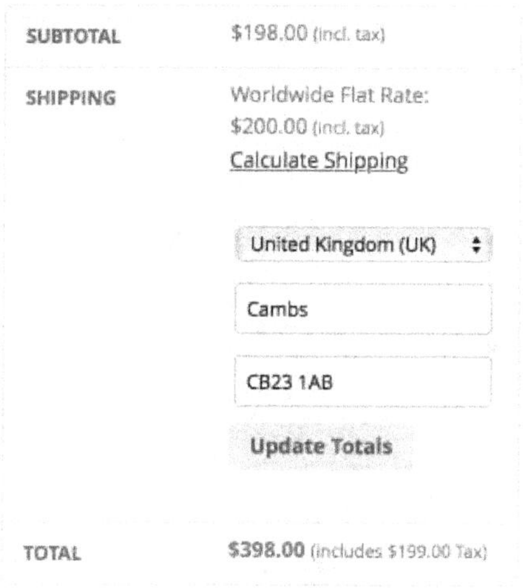

| SUBTOTAL | $198.00 (incl. tax) |
| SHIPPING | Worldwide Flat Rate: $200.00 (incl. tax) |

Calculate Shipping

United Kingdom (UK) ⬍

Cambs

CB23 1AB

Update Totals

| TOTAL | **$398.00** (includes $199.00 Tax) |

CHAPTER 17
PERMALINKS

P ermalink settings can be found at **Woocommerce dash-board > Settings > Permalinks**

From here you can configure the URL structure for your shop and product pages.

Taxonomy Permalinks

There are 3 settings which control the bases of your categories, terms, and attributes:

Product category base	product-category	
Product tag base	product-tag	
Product attribute base		/attribute-name/attribute/

The default category base is **product-category**. An example would be **yourdomain.com/product-category/category-name.**

The default tag base is **product-tag**. An example would be **yourdomain.com/product-tag/tag-name.**

Product attribute base slug will optionally use a custom base before /attribute-name/attribute/ (ex: /size/medium or /color/ blue). Product Permalinks These settings control the permalinks used for products:

Product Permalinks

These settings control the permalinks used for products:

Product Permalinks

These settings control the permalinks used specifically for products.

	Default	https://local.wordpress.dev/product/sample-product/	
	Shop base	https://local.wordpress.dev/shop/sample-product/	
	Shop base with category	https://local.wordpress.dev/shop/product-category/sample-product/	
•	Custom Base	/shop	Enter a custom base to use. A base must be set or WordPress will use default instead.

If you're not using pretty permalinks, 'default' will be the only option available to you and will use ID-based URLs. Example, **yourdomain.com/?product=111**. If you are using pretty **permalinks, the default will be yourdomain.com/product/product-name**.

The other options allow you to prepend the product permalinks with something customs, such as the shop page name, or a completely custom permalink you define.

Note: The product custom base should not conflict with the taxonomy permalink bases. If you set the product base to 'shop' for example, you should not set the product category base to 'shop' too as this will not be unique and will conflict. WordPress requires something unique so it can distinguish categories from products.

CHAPTER 18
WOOCOMMERCE CURRENCY

Woocommerce uses USD as the standard currency. Woocommerce only allows one currency at a time however, If you like to use multiple currencies in your shop then you can purchase Woocommerce currency converter plugin and configure it according to your needs.

Some of the Multi-Currency plugins which I recommend:

1. WooCommerce Multi-Currency
2. MultilingualPress

Currency Settings

To change the Currency of your online store navigate to **WooCommerce > Settings > General > Currency Options** and select your desired currency from the Currency drop-down menu.

Currency Options

The following options affect how prices are displayed on the frontend.

Currency	❓	Swedish krona (kr) ▾
Currency Position	❓	Right (99.99kr) ▾
Thousand Separator	❓	.
Decimal Separator	❓	,
Number of Decimals	❓	2

1. **Currency** – Choose the currency the store will be priced in.
2. **Currency Position** – Choose whether the currency symbol is placed to the left or right of the price.
3. **Thousand Separator** – Choose the character to use for the thousand separators.
4. **Decimal Separator** – Choose the character to use for the decimal separator.
5. **Number of Decimals** – Choose the number of digits to appear after the decimal separator.

CHAPTER 19
COUPONS

C oupons are a great way to offer discounts and rewards to your customers and can help promote sales across your shop.

If you want to use coupons with WooCommerce, you first need to enable them in WooCommerce. Go to: WooCommerce > Settings > General and tick the checkbox to Enable the use of coupons. Then Save Changes.

If you want to generate thousands of coupons automatically with one or two clicks then I recommend installing "Coupon Generator for WooCommerce plugin".

Adding a coupon

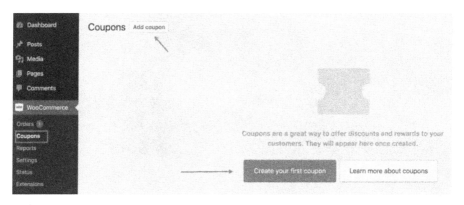

To add a coupon:

1. Go to: **WooCommerce > Coupons.**
2. Create a new coupon by selecting **Add Coupon.** Or hover over an existing one to **Edit.** Enter these fields
3. **Coupon code** – Code used by the customer to apply the coupon. Must be unique as it's used as an identifier.
4. **Description** (optional) — Info about the coupon, e.g., Dates in effect, promotion, compensation, ticket number. For internal use.

Add new coupon

Coupon code

Description (optional)

Coupon data ▲

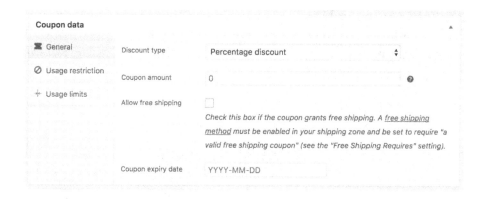

Under Coupon Data, there are three sections you can use to add restrictions and limits for the coupon: **General, Usage Restriction,** and **Usage Limits**.

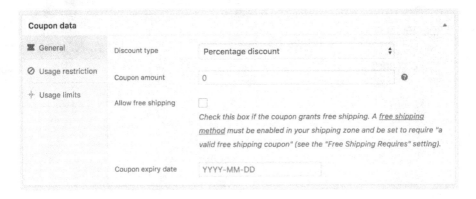

Discount type

1. **Percentage discount** – A percentage discount for selected products only. For example, if the cart contains three (3) t-shirts @ $20 each = $60, a coupon for 10% off applies a discount of $6.
2. **Fixed cart discount** – A fixed total discount for the entire cart. For example, if the cart contains three (3) t-shirts @ $20 each = $60, a coupon for $10 off gives a discount of $10.
3. **Fixed product discount** – A fixed total discount for selected products only. The customer receives a set amount of discount per item. For example, three (3) t-shirts @ $20 each with a coupon for $10 off applies a discount of $30.

Coupon amount – Fixed value or percentage, depending on the discount type you choose. Entered without a currency unit or a percent sign, which are added automatically, e.g., Enter '10' for £10 or 10%.

Allow free shipping – Removes shipping cost when the coupon is used. Requires Free Shipping to be enabled.

Coupon expiry date – Date the coupon should expire and can no longer be used. Expiry happens at 12:00 am or 00:00 on the date chosen. If you want a coupon to be valid through Christmas Day but invalid the moment Christmas is over, set the expiration date to YYYY-12-26 as it will expire on YYYY-12-26 00:00. It uses your site's time zone setting at Settings > General > Timezone in WordPress.

Usage Restriction

1. **Minimum spend** – Allows you to set the minimum subtotal needed to use the coupon. Note: The sum of the cart subtotal + tax is used to determine the minimum amount.
2. **Maximum spend** – Allows you to set the maximum subtotal allowed when using the coupon.
3. **Individual use only** – Tick the box if you don't want this coupon to be used in combination with other coupons.
4. **Exclude sale items** – Tick the box if you don't want this coupon to apply to products on sale. Per-cart coupons do not work if a sale item is added afterward.
5. **Products** – Products that the coupon will be applied

to, or that need to be in the cart in order for the "Fixed cart discount" to be applied.

6. **Exclude products** – Products that the coupon will not be applied to, or that cannot be in the cart in order for the "Fixed cart discount" to be applied.

7. **Product categories** – Product categories that the coupon will be applied to, or that need to be in the cart in order for the "Fixed cart discount" to be applied.

8. **Exclude categories** – Product categories that the coupon will not be applied to, or that cannot be in the cart in order for the "Fixed cart discount" to be applied.

9. **Allowed Emails/Email restrictions** – Email address or addresses that can use a coupon. Verified against customer's billing email. WooCommerce 3.4+ also allows you to include a wildcard character (*) to match multiple email addresses, for example, `*@gmail.com` would make any Gmail address.

Usage Limits

1. **Usage limit per coupon** – How many times a coupon can be used by all customers before being invalid.

2. **Limit usage to X items** – How many items the coupon can be applied to before being invalid. This field is only displayed if there are one or more products that the coupon can be used with, and is configured

under the Usage Restrictions.

3. **Usage limit per user** – How many times a coupon can be used by each customer before being invalid for that customer.

Once you've configured all settings, select Publish and your coupon is ready to use.

Sending Coupons

Once coupons are published, go ahead and make available to customers: Copy the title and send, advertise it via email, social media and onsite banners.

CHAPTER 20
USER ROLES

WooCommerce registers two user roles once acti-vated, and grants additional capabilities to the **Admin:**

1. manage_woocommerce for WooCommerce Settings
2. view_woocommerce_reports

Customer Role

When a user registers via the checkout or signup process, they become customers.

Customers:

1. Have read access only for most capacities. This is the equivalent status to a normal blog subscriber.
2. Can edit their own account information.
3. View past/present orders.

Shop Manager Role

Shop Manager is a role you can give someone to manage the shop without making them an admin. They have all the rights a customer has, and are granted the main capabilities:

1. **manage_woocommerce:** Gives shop managers the option to manage all settings within WooCommerce, and create/edit products.

2. **view_woocommerce_reports**: Gives them access to all WooCommerce reports.

CHAPTER 21
SHIPPING CLASSES

S hipping classes can be used to group products of similar type and used by some shipping methods, such as Flat Rate Shipping, to provide different rates to different classes of product.

For example, with shipping classes and Flat Rate Shipping, it's possible to create different flat rate costs for different product types, like bulky items and small items.

Adding Shipping Classes

◆ Navigate to: **WooCommerce > Settings > Shipping > Shipping Classes.**

Shipping class	Slug	Description	Product count
Bulky	bulky	For heavier items requiring more postage	0
Discount	discount	For special offers	0
Lightweight	light	For smaller items requiring less postage	0
Poster Pack	poster-pack	For poster tubes	0

Shipping zones | Shipping options | **Shipping classes** | Free shipping (legacy)

Shipping classes ❓

Save shipping classes   Add shipping class

◆ **Click** the **Add Shipping Class** button beneath the table. A new row appears.

◆ **Enter** a **Shipping Class Name** and description. Slug (unique identifier) can be left blank and auto-generated, or you can enter one.

◆ **Save Shipping Classes.**

Edit and Delete Shipping Classes

To edit or remove a shipping class:

◆ **Hover** over **Shipping Class Name**. Options appear.
◆ **Click Edit** to revise the name, slug or description. Or click **Remove** to delete the shipping class.

◆ **Save Shipping Classes.**

Assign Shipping Classes to Products

To apply these rates to a specific class of products (e.g., bulky or heavy items), you need to assign them.

◆ Go to: **WooCommerce > Products**.
◆ **Select** the product, and click **Edit**.

◆ Go to **Shipping**, and **select** the **Shipping Class** from the dropdown.

Each product can have one shipping class.

◆ **Update** the product to save changes.

Bulk-Edit Shipping Classes

To bulk-edit shipping classes:

◆ Go to: **WooCommerce > Products.**

◆ **Select the products** you want to edit by ticking boxes on the left-hand side.

◆ **Select Edit** from the Bulk Actions dropdown, then **Apply**. A new screen appears.

◆ **Select** a shipping class from the dropdown.

◆ **Update** to save changes.

CHAPTER 22
UP-SELLS, CROSS-SELLS & RELATED PRODUCTS

P roducts can be Related to each other in three ways: Up-Sells, Cross-Sells or by having the same tags or categories.

To add an up-sell or cross-sell to a product:

1. Go to WooCommerce > Products and select the product on which you'd like to show an up-sell or cross-sell.
2. Scroll down to the Product Data panel. 3
3. Select the Linked Products tab on the left menu.
4. Add the product you wish to link to by searching for it.
5. Update.

Note: related products, up-sells and cross-sells are all sorted randomly.

Up-Sells

Up-sells are products that you recommend instead of the currently viewed product.

They are typically products that are more profitable or better quality or more expensive. Depending on your theme template, these products display on the single product page underneath the product's description.

Up-sells (user-defined) show on the product page.

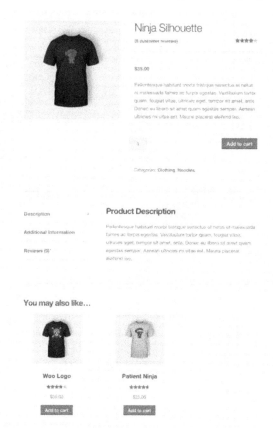

Cross-Sells

Cross-sells are products that you promote in the cart, based on the current product.

They are typically complementary items. For example, if you are selling a laptop, cross-sells might be a protective case or stickers or a special adapter. Or if you're selling a ninja t-shirt, they could be a ninja hoodie and ninja socks.

Depending on your theme template, they display on the cart page underneath the cart products table with a thumbnail image.

Cross-sells (user-defined) show on the cart page.

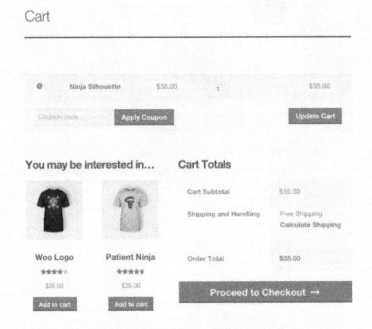

Related Products

Related Products is a section on some templates that pulls products from your store that share the same tags or categories as the current product.

These products cannot be specified in the admin but can be influenced by grouping similar products in the same category or by using the same tags.

Related products (automatic) also show on the product page.

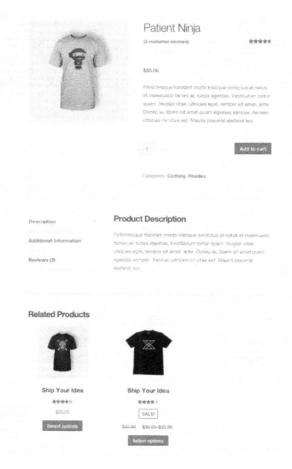

CHAPTER 23
SPEED OPTIMIZATION

WooCommerce stores are still WordPress websites. However, running a store is different from other niches. Given this, let's take a look at shaving every single millisecond you can out of your loading times, focused on your e-commerce storefront.

Compress and Resize Your Product Images

Images are a key component of any modern website but are even more important for online stores. Customers have so many options for buying products online, leveraging every edge is vital. High-quality shots can help differentiate you from other e-commerce sites.

However, detailed product photography means big file sizes. Including multiple images for each product will also bump up the overall file size. Given this, it's important to 'compress' your product images to reduce both file size and loading times, without impacting front-end quality. A great solution for this is TinyPNG:

However, if you have an image-heavy site, automating the process using a plugin such as WP Smush plugin makes more sense. This solution is good due to its user-friendly interface and built-in image resizing features:

Once you install and activate the plugin, you'll come to a quick setup window:

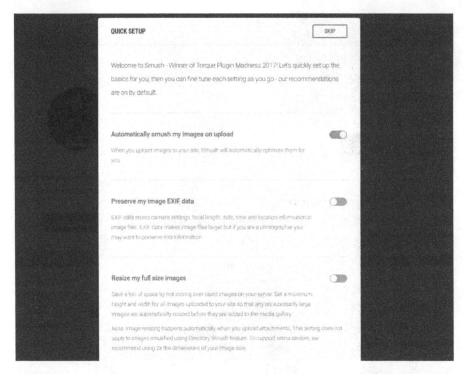

You'll notice the image compression feature is turned on by default. However, you'll also want to turn on the option of reading Resize my full-size images:

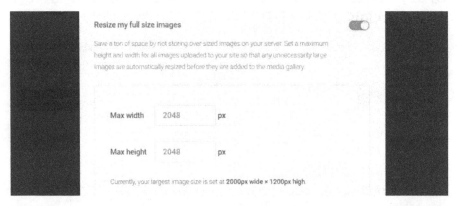

This feature makes sure none of the images you upload have unnecessarily large dimensions. For example, displaying full-resolution images is pointless if your site only displays smaller images throughout. By enabling this option, you're reducing the file size even further, which translates to faster loading times. Of course, you should experiment with the optimal resolution for your WooCommerce product images, but make sure to leave the feature enabled.

Ideally, you'll set up an image optimization plugin as soon as you launch your store. If you haven't optimized every image on your site yet, the BULK SMUSH feature (found via the Smush tab within WordPress), lets you do this efficiently:

However, a major downside to the free version of the plugin is the file size limitation of 1 MB. However, you do get to optimize an unlimited number of images, which isn't found in most similar plugins. If you're regularly dealing with heftier images than this, you may want to invest in a premium image optimization plugin.

Clean Up Your Database Regularly

As you may know, your entire WordPress site is stored in a database. A standard WordPress website accumulates data as time goes by, including post drafts, trashed pages, deleted comments, and more. WooCommerce sites also have product pages, tags, categories, among other data.

Ultimately, this means you may need to clean up your database more often than with other types of websites. While you shouldn't expect miracles, every optimization technique helps.

Fortunately, there are plenty of database optimization plugins to choose from. A popular choice is WP-Optimize, which is very simple to use:

Once you activate the plugin, a new WP-Optimize tab will appear on your WordPress dashboard. Here, you'll see a list of the tables the plugin can optimize, and how many entries it will clean up within each of them:

In our experience, it's usually safe to optimize all of your tables at once. However, we still recommend you do a full backup of your website beforehand, just in case the worst happens.

Use a Content Delivery Network (CDN)

One of the factors that determine how long your WooCommerce store takes to load is the distance between your visitors and your server. The larger the distance, the longer your website will take to load, even over high-speed internet connections.

The best way to deal with this issue is to use a CDN. What these services do is store (or cache) copies of your website on data centers around the world. Then, when someone tries to access your site, your CDN will redirect them to the nearest copy of it, so to speak.

This approach enables you to cut down loading times across the board. However, this kind of service doesn't often come for free – although companies such as Cloudflare offer limited free tiers:

The Cloudflare free plan isn't as rapid as other premium CDNs, although it's easy to integrate with WordPress and WooCommerce, and a breeze to use (especially with a host that integrates the service).

If you have a higher budget, Cloudflare's premium plans also include built-in image optimization. This means they're especially well-suited for WooCommerce websites with a lot of product images – and they can reduce your loading times even further.

Of course, there are plenty of other CDN solutions to consider, so it's worth shopping around to find the right solution for you.

Set Up a Caching Solution

Caching is a great step for store owners who want to easily and affordably speed up their store.

Essentially, a caching plugin creates and stores a static version of your store so when a customer returns to shop with you again, they will see a cached version of your product pages.

The great thing about WordPress caching is that it occurs without the customer knowing that it's happening; that they're seeing the content they've already previously downloaded. Caching minimizes the amount of data that is sent between the customer's browser, the WordPress database and the web server, which means faster loading times.

When using a caching plugin for your WooCommerce site, make sure you exclude these pages from the cache:

Cart
  My Account
  Checkout

These pages, as well as other elements like cart widgets, need to remain dynamic since they display information specific to the current customer.

Since your cart and checkout pages can't be cached but are crucial to conversions, it's imperative that you pay special attention to their speed. It's important that you do everything you can to streamline these pages as best you can, removing any unnecessary assets.

WP Rocket is fully compatible with WooCommerce, so you don't need to manually exclude these pages – WP Rocket automatically detects all WooCommerce pages and doesn't cache them. However, it is recommended that you avoid minifying JavaScript files.

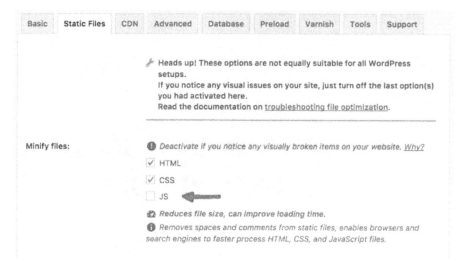

Inadvertently caching dynamic pages in your store can result in the customer seeing unexpected results, such as content they had previously viewed instead of new products they've added to their cart. So even if you think caching is working as it should be, it's important to test your WooCommerce cache setup once you've configured your caching plugin to ensure it's working as expected.

CHAPTER 24
INTRODUCING TO SOME POWERFUL PLUGINS

I n this chapter, I will introduce you to some of the powerful plugins which I used when I created my first online store.

Marketplace Plugins

If you like to change your store as a Multi-Vendor Marketplace where anyone can buy and trade online then some of the best plugins are:

DOKAN- The plugin is developed by devs. They have a free version as well as the premium version the free version have very limited features but in their premium plugin, they have a lot's of features which you need as a Marketplace owner. The quality of their plugin and support is really good.

Woocommerce Marketplace- The marketplace plugin is free but they have some paid add-ons like WC-Membership, WC-Groups & Staffs, WC-Analysis, WC-Ultimate, etc.. As comparing to the price of other marketplace plugin Wclover's plugins are cheap and give a lot of features out of the box.

WC-Vendors, WC-Marketplace, YITH Multi-vendor - These plugins have their free versions as well as paid versions but they

Lack lot's of features as compared to DOKAN and WC-Market-place. WC-Vendors plugin is the best option if you're developing a B2B Multi-Vendor Marketplace.

Sales and Marketing Plugins

Sales is an important factor of an online store, to generate more sales your store need to be well optimized for sales and conversions, these plugins will help you to optimize your store for sales:

Beeketing - Marketing Automation to Boost Sales

This plugin helps you to convert more visitors into revenue through automating marketing using AI, with Beeketing you can track your customer's behaviors, Analyse & learn customers interest on your store and boost your checkout and conversion rates.

List of Beeketing Apps

1. **Better Coupon Box** - this app helps you to convert new visitors into email subscribers or social followers, Encourage customers to purchase by giving away coupon codes, Prevent site abandonment with Exit-Intent Popups
2. **Countdown Cart** - Sales countdown timer to create urgency for discount deals, Stock countdown bar to display the limited stock of products, Social proof widget to show how many people have viewed or bought an item
3. **Sales Pop** - Show recent order notifications to increase customer buying confidence, Let app sync your order list, or create custom notifications of your choice, Create social proof, a sense of a busy store, and brand trust

4. **Boost Sales** - Upsell related items & Cross-sell product bundles at discount prices, Last-step up-sell at cart page to motivate customers to spend more, Automated upsells & cross-sells backed by AI to save your time.

5. **Check out Boost** - Offer free gifts, discount, or free shipping codes to increase checkout rate, Boost Facebook / Twitter shares and social referral traffic, Countdown-timer and Exit-intent offers to prevent abandoned carts

6. **Personalized Recommendation** - 5+ types of product recommendation sliders on all pages, Product templates are 100% customizable and responsive on mobile devices, Let the app automate recommendations or create your cross-sell rules.

7. **Mailbot Email Marketing** - Send personalized follow-up emails automatically, Advanced customer segmentation to trigger campaigns, Cart abandonment, win-back and coupon reward campaigns to nurture loyal customers

8. **Quick Facebook Chat** - Install a live Facebook chat widget on your store, Support customers anytime, anywhere via Messenger accounts, Increase Facebook page likes via the live chat widget

XL-Sales Triggers Plugin

XL WooCommerce Sales Triggers Boosts Conversion Rate By Deploying 7 Power Packed Conversion Triggers

XL-Sales Triggers plugin is a premium plugin, you have to purchase the license, install the plugin and activate the triggers you'd like to use.

List of available sales triggers:

1. Display a countdown Timer to create urgency

2. Show the items left in stock to Induce Scarcity
3. Display potential savings to trigger loss aversion
4. Share the most recent sales activity to activate social proof.
5. Give a bullet-proof guarantee to show your commitment.
6. Display the satisfaction rate to amp up confidence
7. Highlight the store's best sellers to reduce anxiety.

Google Product feed plugin

The Google Product Feed plugin helps you to create a feed so that you can send your product details to the Google Merchant Center [GMC]. This is prerequisite for setting up Google Shopping Product Ads and Google Remarketing Ads, You can choose what fields you want to include in your product feed, based on Google policies. After filling everything in, you will end up with an automated feed with all your product information in the correct format for Google.

Furthermore, these extensions allow you to capture data which is required by Google by using the plugin's additional data entry fields. You will have to own a Google Merchant Center Account to use this plug-in. With it, your company products will appear in Google Shopping. This extension is also compatible with the Product CSV Import Suite which allows you to bulk import product feed information.

WooCommerce Google Analytics Pro

Google Analytics hardly needs any introduction. It is a powerful web analytics tool used for tracking page views and visitors on your website. The WooCommerce Google Analytics Pro plugin blends with Google Analytics accounts. You can use it for tracking the e-commerce events and it comes with top-notch event tracking features including purchase and coupon usage, reviews, etc. WooCommerce Google Analytics Pro basically boosts integration between your Google Analytics account and WooCommerce store. This helps you tweak strategies and fetch more revenues. There are a free version and a Pro variant. The latter offers better and accurate conversion rate tracking. It gives you clear insight into vita metrics like conversion rate, sales by category or product and so on. It also lets you monitor the sales process.

Facebook for WooCommerce plugin

This plugin is ideal for business owners that already have an existing profile on other social network sites that are popular and want to maximize sales and get more customers. This Plug-in creates a shop tab on the left side of the FB page and integrates with FB. Through that tab, buyers would be able to view and purchase products. Once they are ready to complete their order, they would be redirected to your website in order to check out.

Yoast SEO for WooCommerce plugin

Yoast SEO is one of the top SEO plugins for WordPress and it now has a WooCommerce plugin. If you're aiming for the best SEO optimization, this plugin will not disappoint you. It comes with different tools, it allows you to share your products on social media channels in an easier and better way, and it also helps you in removing things you don't want from the sitemap. This plug-in would be helping you enhance the basic functions in the backend.

AffiliateWP plugin

With time, more online businesses are resorting to the method known as affiliate marketing. In this marketing technique, you can allow other shops to sell your products or refer their clients to your website. These shops will get a percentage of the price of the product. This will result in more clients and thus more revenue for you. You can deploy an affiliate system to handle such affiliate accounts. It helps track traffic sent by those affiliates to your site. One such excellent plug-in compatible with WooCommerce is AffiliateWP.

AffiliateWP is user-friendly and comes with a 30-day money back assurance. It helps fetch more traffic to your website. It also makes sure that you get higher visibility of activity of affiliates as well. Eventually, it leads to more sales.

WooCommerce Multilingual plugin

This plugin helps you to translate your product and other WooCommerce pages into other languages. It also helps your shoppers feel comfortable navigating your site and lets them view product information in the language that works for them.

Showing product info in the language your visitors are most comfortable in makes a big difference to your bottom line.

WooCommerce Currency Switcher plugin

Using a currency converter like WooCommerce Currency Switcher makes it easy for your shoppers to see what they're paying in their own country's currency. It's a small thing that can make a big difference in a shopper's decision to buy.

With this free WooCommerce plugin, you can even set fixed minimum amounts for free shipping offers. This means that you won't be using all of your profits to cover international shipping costs.

This plugin helps your shoppers to switch currencies and get rates converted in real time.

CHAPTER 25
CHILD THEME CREATION

I n this chapter, we will discuss how you can style your WooCommerce store using themes. Then we'll discuss how we can create our own child theme in just a few steps.

In this chapter, we will use the Storefront theme to create a child theme, although you can use any theme as a base. Storefront theme a quite professional looking theme and it's an official Woocommerce theme, built specifically to integrate with the plugin. It looks compelling right out of the box, with a simple and clean design that puts the focus on your products.

If you want to customize the appearance of your WooCommerce store to match your exact vision then the best solution is to create a WooCommerce child theme. A child theme enables you to make changes to your original theme without editing it directly. This simplifies the process of customizing your store's appearance and eliminates potential risk to your theme and store.

I highly recommend that you create a backup of your site before you proceed any further. This will keep your store safe if something breaks during the development process. It's also smart to use a staging environment for creating and tweaking your child theme. Once you've taken these security precautions, you can proceed.

Make a Folder for Your WooCommerce Child Theme

The first thing we need to do is to create a folder that will contain your theme. If you're adding the child theme directly to an existing site, the best way to do this is via SFTP. You can do this using a free application like **FileZilla**.

Once you have the program up and running, log in to your site with your hosting credentials. Then, you'll need to navigate to the **wp-content/themes/** folder. This is where your site's themes are installed. All you need to do is create a new folder within this one:

When creating a child theme, it's best to give it a name that reflects the parent.

For example, we're making a child theme for Storefront, so we'll name our folder storefront-child.

The first thing you'll need to create and place in this folder is a simple text file called **functions.php**. This is an important core file that helps to dictate how your site looks and acts. However, most child themes can use the functions contained in the parent theme's file and don't need their own.

129

For that reason, this file can be left blank for now. Simply create a text file with the name **functions.php**, and save it in your child theme's folder:

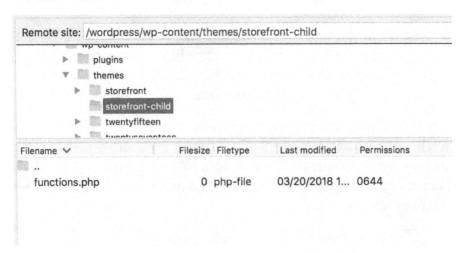

Your theme is now almost ready to be activated and used. First, however, it will need a stylesheet.

Creating Your Child Theme's Stylesheet

The next file you need to create is your theme's Cascading Style Sheet (CSS). This file defines the styles that will be applied to your site's pages and content. In other words, it enables you to specify the look of individual elements on your site. When people talk about updating styles, they're usually referring to updating a site's CSS file.

Your parent theme will already contain a stylesheet, but a child theme's CSS can be used to override those styles. We'll look at how exactly this works later on. For now, you'll just need to create the CSS file. To do this, once again add a text file to your wp-content/themes/storefront-child folder (or whatever name you used for your own child theme). This one should be called style.css:

You'll also need to add some basic information. Add these following snippet into your new style.css file:

/* Theme Name: Storefront Child
Theme URI: http://example.com/storefront-child/
Description: My first WooCommerce child theme
Author: Your Name
Author URI: http://example.com
Version: 1.0.0
License: GNU General Public License v2 or later
License URI: http://www.gnu.org/licenses/gpl-2.0.html */

These are the details about your theme that you'll see when viewing it in a theme directory, or in your WordPress dashboard. Feel free to replace the placeholder information with information more specific to you and your theme.

Configure the Child Theme to Inherit the Parent Theme's Styles

As I mentioned earlier, you'll want your child theme to use the parent theme's default styles. However, you'll also need to override the styles you want to change. This might sound complex – and CSS can indeed get tricky – but at its core, the child will always use the parent theme's styles unless it specifically contains a replacement.

For example, let's say your parent theme defines the style for h1 header elements as 20px and red. If the child's style.css file does not contain an entry for H1 headers, then the parent style will be applied to all H1 content. However, if we were to add an H1 style to the child's stylesheet that defined these headings as 18px and blue, this will override the parent's directions.

Adding this functionality to your child theme is actually very simple. All you need to do is to reference your parent theme in your child's stylesheet. Simply add the following snippet after the information you pasted into the style.css file earlier:

Template: storefront

This defines the parent theme and will ensure your child theme uses Storefront's styles wherever you have not specified a replacement. If you're creating a child for a different theme, you can simply use its folder's name instead.

Activate the Child Theme

At this point, your child theme is now technically ready. It's configured to work on your site, so let's activate it and see how it looks.

Go to **Appearance > Themes** in your WordPress dashboard, and you'll see your child theme already installed:

Select **Activate** to make it your site's current theme. You can now preview it from the front end:

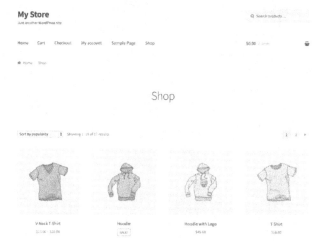

As you can see, it looks exactly the same as the original theme right now. While the child theme is active, all it's doing is pulling in the styles from your parent theme. To customize its appearance, you'll need to get creative with your child theme's stylesheet.

Add Styles to the Child Theme

Finally, it's time to start styling your child theme. Exactly how you do this is up to you, your creativity, and what you want your store to look like. However, let's walk through an example of what you can do.

To illustrate how editing your child theme works, we'll change the look of our store's buttons. At the moment they appear gray with black text, but we could update this styling to make them stand out more:

Open your child theme's style.css file again, and add the following code after the last */ in the file's header:

```
a.button,
   button.button,
   input.button,
   #review_form #submit {
   background: pink;
   color: red;
   }
```

If you save your file and view it on the front end now, you'll see the change in action. The buttons will now be a vibrant pink, with red text:

You can also make changes to your theme's template files. You'll just need to copy the template file you want to alter, such as header.php, from your parent to your child theme folder. However, you'll also need to make some changes to specify which function WordPress uses to reference the template files. This requires that you use the get_stylesheet_directory(); function instead of get_template_directory() to reference your templates. To learn more about how to do this, you can read up about all the templates that WooCommerce uses.

At this point, you have created a WooCommerce child theme! Of course, there's plenty more you can do.

CHAPTER 25
WOOCOMMERCE & GUTENBERG

O n December 6th, 2018 the controversial new editor experience for WordPress v5.0 dropped and it's called Gutenberg. While many are concerned about how it was rolled out I don't think that anyone can deny that Gutenberg is the future of WordPress. That also means that Gutenberg is the future of WooCommerce.

By default there are no blocks bundled with WooCommerce as of WooCommerce 3.5.1 so you'll need to head over to the WooCommerce official site to get WooCommerce Product Blocks. WooCommerce Product Blocks is a free add-on to WooCommerce. To continue along with me you'll need to get the plugin, and install it in your website and then activate it. From there, navigate to a page to start adding products to the site.

Adding a WooCommerce Product with Gutenberg

To get started adding products, start by clicking on the plus in the top left corner of your Gutenberg-powered site. Now type "products" to filter the block options down to the blocks that deal with the products in the store. Then click on the "Products" block.

This block should appear below any content on your page. Now you can choose to show products in a number of different ways. Let's choose to add an individual product to our page to get started. Click "Individual products", which should bring up a search box for you to start searching your products by their names. Once you find the product you want, click on it to add it to the block.

You're not limited to a single product though, you can even add multiple products from a single search. They'll display listed across in a grid fashion by default.

Once you have the products you want to show selected, click done and then make sure you save your page.

In addition to hand-picking products, you can add products from a specific category to a page. If there are sub-categories you can choose which ones you want to display.

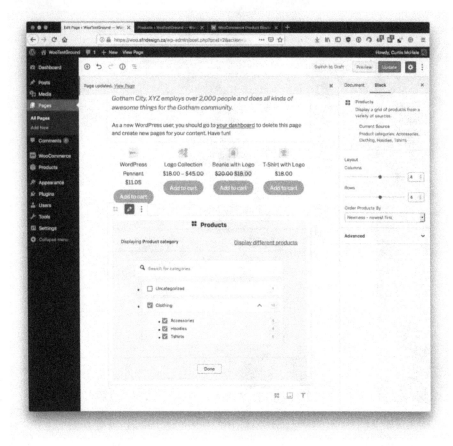

Selecting a category will add every product inside that category to the page.

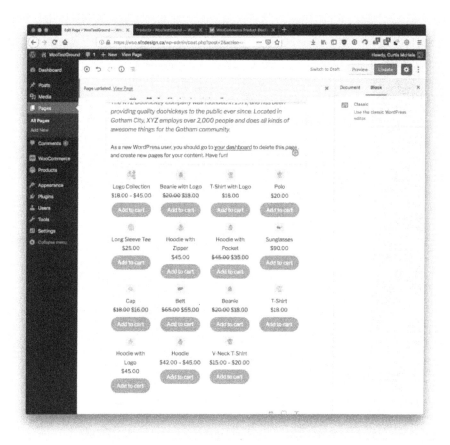

You can also use a Product Block to show products by a specific product attribute. As Valentine's Day approaches, you could use your color product attribute to build a custom page with all the red products you have in the store to suit the season.

Just like the other ways we've looked at showing products, this will add all of the products that match the attribute to your page. You can use a number of attributes like:

1. Products on Sale
2. Best Sellers
3. Featured Products
4. Top-Rated Products

The other block that is available with the WooCommerce Product Blocks plugin allows you to show products by category, which duplicates the functionality of adding products by category with the products block.

Customizing Your WooCommerce Gutenberg Product Block

While we've toured some of the basics of adding product blocks to your content, we haven't taken a look at what the customization options are to maximize how your page looks.

To start, WooCommerce Product Blocks lets you customize the number of products that are shown in both columns and rows.

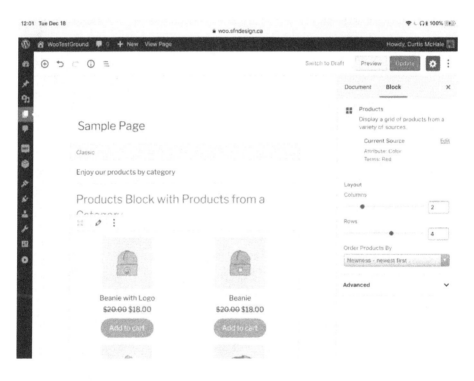

You could leverage this to show a single product on a long form sales page by making your product block only display one item per column. Then you would choose a single product to add to the block.

You can also use the block settings to change the order of your products with the following options available now:

1. Newest – newest first
2. Price – low to high
3. Price – high to low
4. Rating – highest first
5. Sales – most first
6. Title – alphabetical

Finally, under the advanced options, you can add a custom CSS class if you want to do further styling to your block to help it suit your theme. Given the right CSS rules, you could change the layout.

Building a Custom Product Landing Page with WooCommerce and Gutenberg

Now let's take some of the knowledge we've gained about WooCommerce and Gutenberg to build ourselves a long form sales page for a product. You can start by creating a new page giving it a title. I've also added a bit of text to a paragraph block and used the drop cap option found on the right side of our block settings.

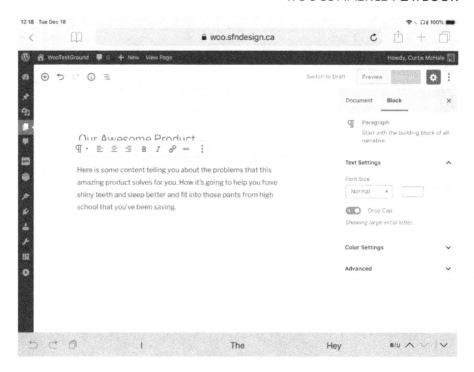

With many long-form sales pages, we'll end up adding the product to the page a few times. You do this to give people the opportunity to purchase your product as soon as they are convinced that it's a good buy for them.

Next, add a product block and choose a single product to add to your page. Then move over to the right side and change the column display to a single product per column. This should give you a large version of the product displayed on the page with an add to cart button just below it.

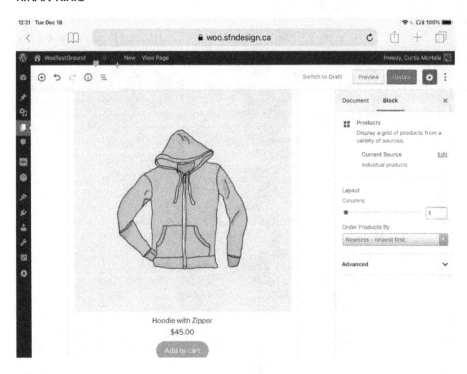

Next, click on the three vertical dots at the top of your product block and choose to "Add to Reusable Blocks." This will let us take the block we've created for ourselves and easily get to the exact settings we already have without needing to go through the hassle of finding the product and changing our column settings again later. Title this block whatever you want and then save the reusable block.

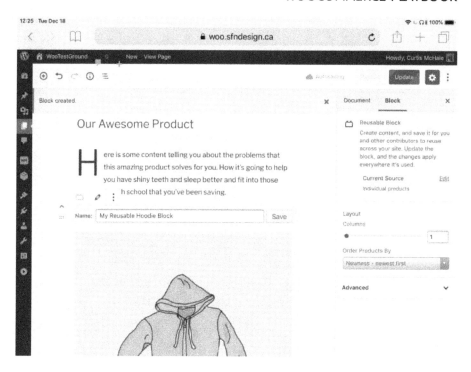

Now we can add some more text to the page which would be used to show the users the benefits of our amazing hoodie. Let's even use the quote block to provide a testimonial from one of the happy hoodie clients.

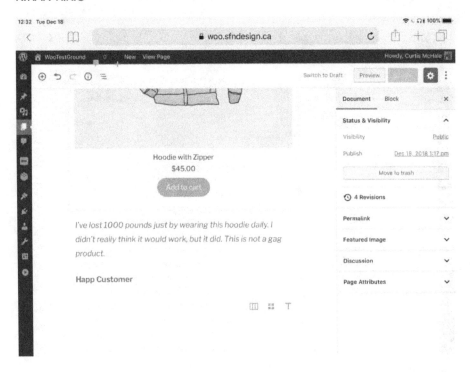

Then you'd normally add some more text showing off the benefits of your product for the users or answering any questions they may have about the product. We can use a column block to do this and answer two questions for our user. We can finish off this page by using our reusable hoodie block to invite the user to purchase our amazing hoodie again.

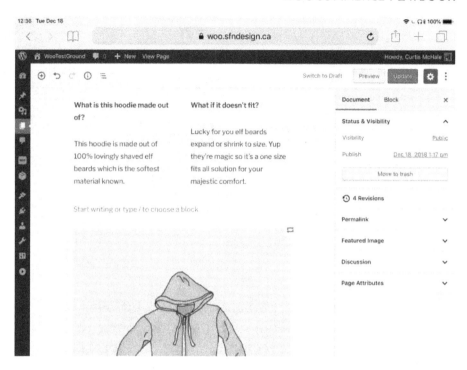

Previously when clients wanted a custom product landing page like this they would have to use some page building plugin. Some of these are decent, but a vast majority are less than desirable on your site. When I compare the experience of Gutenberg to these other page building options, Gutenberg is far more intuitive for my customers to use on their own without needing me to build anything custom for them.

CONCLUSION

P hew!

Right now you're probably feeling a bit overwhelmed. You've just concluded a full-on immersion course in Creating a online store using Woocommerce and Wordpress, and you should feel proud of yourself.

Being overwhelmed is actually a good thing because even though you feel like all that information is a big, your brain is subconciously making inner connections. Right now you know how to create an online store now you have to put your store and your products in front of right audience so that every traffic which you get can be converted to sales. It's better you figureout strengths and weekness of your competators and use it in your marketting strategies.

This book is a playbook. Dont just read it once and go on with business as usual. Keep it handy, and refer to it often. I would strongly suggest spending a week or two implementing one of secrets you learn from this book.

Many people who read this book before it went public wanted to look into their ideas personally, including their startup eCommerce stores and Marketplaces, I did just for my few friends and identify and solve the problems when they face in developing their marketplaces.

Once this book is available to millions, I know it's hard to ac-commmodate everyone who needs a personal help. So I had created something special for the readers of this book. I've opened a website called kiranraj.com you can apply with me personally and I will spend a hour with you over phone and then have my team work with you for a full year to implement the changes you need to make.

And with that.....
I will end this book.
Thank you so much for reading, and I wish you all the sucess you can dream of...

KIRANRAJ KG

◆ ◆ ◆